POCKETS
CATS

D0057724

OCELOT

IVORY PANEL
(8TH CENTURY B.C.)
OF A MAN-EATING LION

BLUE ABYSSINIAN

CATS

Written by
DAVID ALDERTON

PREHISTORIC
SMILODON
SKULL

TORTOISESHELL
AND WHITE
MOTHER AND
KITTEN

CARACAL

DK
DK PUBLISHING

LONDON, NEW YORK,
MELBOURNE, MUNICH, and DELHI

Project editor Elise Bradbury
Art editor Clair Watson
Senior editor Laura Buller
Senior art editor Helen Senior
Production Louise Barratt, Catherine Semark
Picture research Fiona Watson
US editor Jill Hamilton

REVISED EDITION
Project editor Steve Setford
Designer Sarah Crouch
Managing editor Linda Esposito
Managing art editor Jane Thomas
DTP designer Siu Yin Ho
Consultant David Alderton
Production Erica Rosen
US editors Margaret Parrish, Christine Heilman

Second American Edition, 2003
Published in the United States by
DK Publishing, Inc., 375 Hudson Street,
New York, New York 10014

04 05 06 07 08 10 9 8 7 6 5 4

A Cataloging-in-Publication record for the First American Edition of this book
is available from the Library of Congress.

ISBN 0-7894-9590 2

Color reproduction by Colourscan, Singapore
Printed and bound in Italy by L.E.G.O.

See our complete product line at
www.dk.com

CONTENTS

HOW TO USE THIS BOOK

These pages show you how to use *Pockets: Cats*.
The book is divided into several sections. The main
section consists of information about different breeds
of domestic cats as well as many of the wild cats.
There is also an introductory section at the front of
the book, and a reference section at the back. Each
new section begins with a
page that lists what will
follow in that section.

DIFFERENT TYPES OF CATS
The domestic cats in this book are
divided into groups according to
coat length. The wild cats have their
own separate section. Within each
section, there is detailed information
about different species or breeds.

Corner coding

Heading

Introduction

Caption

SIMILAR CATS WITH DIFFERENT COATS

ABYSSINIAN AND SOMALI
THE FIRST ABYSSINIAN CAT was brought to Britain in
1868 by soldiers returning from war in Abyssinia
(now Ethiopia). Abyssinians look so similar to the
cats in ancient Egyptian wall paintings that they are
believed to be related. The Somali breed originated
from long-coated kittens
in Abyssinian litters.

Ticked fur is short, thick, and glossy

BLUE ABYSSINIAN

TRADITIONAL COLOURING
The original Abyssinian is known as the Ruddy, or Usual. It is sometimes called the "rabbit cat" because the reddish-brown ticked color of its coat is like a wild rabbit's. These athletic and lively cats have been popular pets for decades.

TWO-TONE COAT
The Blue Abyssinian used to be very rare, but has now become more common. It has a steel blue-gray coat with an oatmeal colored undercoat. New colors are developed by crossbreeding with other types of cats.

CORNER CODING
The top corners of
the pages in a section
are color coded to
remind you which
section you are in.

SIMILAR CATS WITH
DIFFERENT COATS

LONGHAIRED
CATS

SHORTHAIRED
CATS

THE WORLD'S
WILD CATS

HEADING
The heading describes
the subject of the
page. This page is
about the Abyssinian
and Somali pedigree
cat breeds.

INTRODUCTION
This provides a clear,
general overview of the
subject. After reading
this, you should have
an idea what the pages
are about.

CAPTIONS AND
ANNOTATIONS
Each illustration has a
caption. Annotations, in
italics, point out features of
an illustration and usually
have leader lines.

RUNNING HEADS
These remind you which section you are in. The top of the left-hand page gives the section name. The right-hand page gives the subject. This page on the Abyssinian and Somali breeds is in the Similar Cats with Different Coats section.

FEATURE BOXES
Throughout the book, feature boxes supply extra information. This feature box gives details about the fur color of Abyssinians and Somalis.

FACT BOXES
Many pages have fact boxes. These contain at-a-glance, interesting information about the topic. Fact boxes include specific information about the subject matter that is discussed on the page.

Running head   *Feature box*

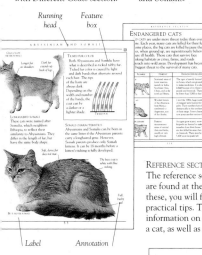

Label   *Annotation*

REFERENCE SECTION
The reference section pages are yellow and are found at the back of the book. On these, you will find useful facts and practical tips. These pages give you information on choosing and caring for a cat, as well as amazing cat records.

LABELS
For extra clarity, many of the pictures have labels. These may give extra information, or identify a picture when it is not obvious from the text.

INDEX
You will find an index at the back of this book. This lists alphabetically every subject and every type of cat that is covered in the rest of the book.

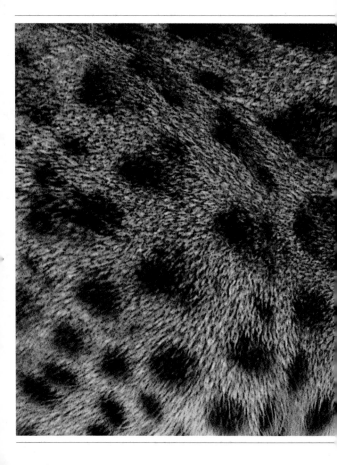

INTRODUCTION
TO CATS

WHAT IS A CAT?

CATS ARE NATURE'S most efficiently designed hunting carnivores. They have powerful bodies, superb vision, and razor-sharp teeth and claws. Most cats are self-reliant, stalking their prey alone in dusk or darkness. One species has also succeeded in living with people and is now kept as a pet around the world.

AFRICAN LION

ANCIENT EGYPTIAN CAT

Short, rounded head

Sandy-brown coat for camouflage

Cats lived near settlements, where they could easily find food.

Strong front legs and muscular neck for catching prey

Sharp claws are kept sheathed when not in use.

HISTORY OF THE DOMESTIC CAT
Wall paintings show that cats were being tamed in ancient Egypt before 2500 B.C. Although the Egyptians forbade the export of their cats, they still spread to ancient Greece by 500 B.C. They were also recorded in India before 100 B.C.

MOTHER AND KITTEN

TYPICAL MAMMAL
Like other mammals, cats are warm-blooded and have a skeleton and a four-chambered heart. The female gives birth to live young and produces milk to feed her kittens.

Loose skin for freedom of movement

Flexible backbone increases length of stride as cat runs.

CAT FACTS
• Cats survive on any meat or fish they can catch. When hungry, even the largest cats will eat insects.

• Australia and Antarctica are the only continents with no native cat species.

• Except for tigers, most wild cats attack people only if they are too old to catch their usual animal prey.

Tail is one-third the length of the body.

Back legs are powered by the largest muscles in the cat's body.

Long, dark hair at tip of tail is used for signaling.

THE HUNTER
Virtually everything about a cat, including the domestic cat, is designed for hunting. Cats are lithe, intelligent, and strong, and react with lightning speed. A cat approaches its prey using stealth and camouflage, then overpowers its victim. Lions are the only cats that hunt in groups.

THE FIRST CATS

A SMALL CARNIVORE similar to a pine marten hunted in the trees of prehistoric forests 50 million years ago. This was the cat's most distant ancestor. Some 12 million years ago, the first true cats evolved. Many of these first species of cat no longer exist.

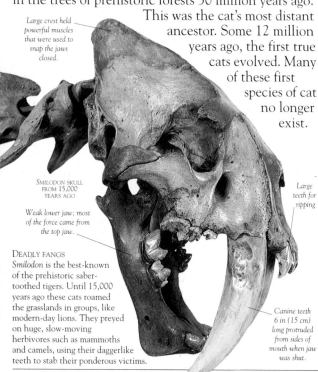

Large crest held powerful muscles that were used to snap the jaws closed.

SMILODON SKULL FROM 15,000 YEARS AGO

Weak lower jaw; most of the force came from the top jaw.

Large teeth for ripping

Canine teeth 6 in (15 cm) long protruded from sides of mouth when jaw was shut.

DEADLY FANGS
Smilodon is the best-known of the prehistoric saber-toothed tigers. Until 15,000 years ago these cats roamed the grasslands in groups, like modern-day lions. They preyed on huge, slow-moving herbivores such as mammoths and camels, using their daggerlike teeth to stab their ponderous victims.

SABER-TOOTH KILL

Mammoth struggling in sticky tar

RANCHO LA BREA TAR PIT, CALIFORNIA
The remains of over 2,000 *Smilodon* cats have been found in this US site. Over centuries, saber-tooths came here to prey on animals trapped in tar and then became stuck themselves.

WHERE THEY LIVED
Smilodon lived mainly in North America. Similar cats known as *Megantereon* ranged across northern India, Africa, and the Mediterranean coast, as well as North America. More recently, lions and giant cheetahs roamed Europe.

THE EVOLUTION OF CATS
All carnivores evolved from a common ancestor that lived 65 million years ago. The cat family (Felidae) split off from the hyenas, which are their closest relatives, 40 million years ago. The mongoose and genet families are also related to cats.

[Evolution chart with timeline in millions of years ago: 65, 57, 37, 24, 5, 0 — CARNIVORES — HERPESTIDAE, FELIDAE, HYAENIDAE, VIVERRIDAE — INDIAN MONGOOSE, JAGUAR, SPOTTED HYENA, COMMON GENET]

SMILODON RECONSTRUCTION FROM FOSSIL REMAINS

Smilodon *was about the same size as a modern lion.*

Exact color is unknown.

TYPES OF CAT

THE CAT FAMILY includes about 39 species of cat, from the tiger to the domestic cat. Depending on whether they live in the desert, savannah, forest, jungle – or in our homes – the different types of cat vary widely in size, color, markings, and way of life.

MOUNTAIN DWELLER
The adaptable bobcat lives in a wide range of North American habitats, from swamps to snowy mountains. Bobcats are one of only two types of wild cat with short, stumpy tails. They are still hunted for their fur.

DOMESTIC CATS
One of the smallest members of the cat family, the domestic cat is found nearly everywhere. These cats still sometimes interbreed with their ancestors, the wildcats.

Massive paws can strike a fatal blow.

RED POINT
BRITISH
SHORTHAIR

INDIAN
TIGER

UNIQUE GRASSLANDS HUNTER
The cheetah is classed in a distinct group from all the other cats because it is best at running rather than leaping. Its unrivaled speed and acute vision have evolved for hunting in open country.

CLIMBING CATS
Some types of cat specialize in climbing. Leopards are the biggest of these excellent climbers. They will scale a tree and then ambush unsuspecting animals that pass underneath. Some small cats regularly hunt birds and lizards in the leafy treetops of the forest.

LEOPARD

Leopards are found in Asia and Africa.

The Indian tiger can weigh up to 575 lb (260 kg).

Unique striped pattern camouflages the animal in forests.

BIG CAT
The tiger is the largest and most powerful of all the cats. Tigers can live from the rainforests of Southeast Asia to the harsh cold of Siberia. Siberian tigers are the biggest of the group. Tigers cannot run quickly for long, but are strong enough to tackle large prey. They are also good swimmers.

CAT ANATOMY

ALL CATS ARE AGILE and athletic predators. Their
bodies are powerful and flexible, specially designed
for running, jumping, and climbing. Some types of cat
even excel at swimming. Superb hunters, cats first
swiftly chase and then overpower prey with
their strength. Sharp teeth
are used to finish
off the catch.

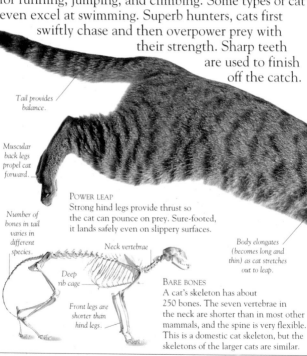

*Tail provides
balance.*

*Muscular
back legs
propel cat
forward.*

POWER LEAP
Strong hind legs provide thrust so
the cat can pounce on prey. Sure-footed,
it lands safely even on slippery surfaces.

*Number of
bones in tail
varies in
different
species.*

Neck vertebrae

*Deep
rib cage*

*Front legs are
shorter than
hind legs.*

*Body elongates
(becomes long and
thin) as cat stretches
out to leap.*

BARE BONES
A cat's skeleton has about
250 bones. The seven vertebrae in
the neck are shorter than in most other
mammals, and the spine is very flexible.
This is a domestic cat skeleton, but the
skeletons of the larger cats are similar.

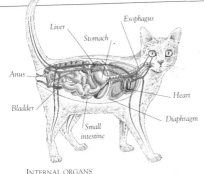

Liver
Esophagus
Stomach
Anus
Bladder
Heart
Diaphragm
Small
intestine

INTERNAL ORGANS
The intestines of a cat are short and simple since they need to digest only meat and not plants. Most of the nutrients from the food are absorbed in the small intestine.

Powerful jaw muscles attach to side of skull.

Incisor, or biting, teeth

Canine teeth to kill prey

Carnassial teeth tear prey apart.

Front legs take most of the impact of landing.

Pads on the feet help cushion the cat as it lands.

CAT SKULL
A cat's skull is large compared to the size of its body. The eye sockets are big to allow for broad range of vision. The jaws are short and strong. All of a cat's teeth are sharp and scissorlike for tearing and cutting, rather than flat, like a human's, for crushing.

Heads and faces

With its powerful eyesight, acute hearing, strong jaws, and sharp teeth, a cat's head is designed for efficiently killing prey. To be an effective hunter, a cat must be able to think quickly, so cats have quite large brains. Domestic cats share these qualities with their wild relatives. However, selective breeding (when cats are specially bred by humans to develop particular characteristics) has created a huge variety of head shapes and facial features. Cats' faces may also change as they age.

HISTORICAL SIAMESE
A breed's appearance can change over time. This prize-winning Siamese from the early 1900s has a rounded face far removed from today's Siamese cats.

Adult tomcats develop jowls that look like a double chin.

Nose is puglike, sometimes causing breathing difficulties.

Siamese cats have large, pointed ears with wide bases.

ROUND FACE
It is often possible to identify a domestic breed by its face shape. The British Shorthair has a distinctly rounded face and large head. Its ears are set wide apart.

FLAT FACE
The facial shape of the Persian, the oldest of the longhaired breeds, has changed dramatically over the last hundred years. Today Persians have extremely flat faces.

WEDGE FACE
A triangular face is now typical of Siamese and Oriental cats. In cat shows, a Siamese is judged by its slender, angular head and its almond-shaped eyes.

THE KING OF THE BEASTS

A lion has the most recognizable head of any type of cat. The unique mane of the male lion makes it the only member of the cat family that can easily be distinguished from the female of the same species. The purpose of the lion's mane is probably to make him look more threatening. Only mature males are able to grow a mane – neutered males cannot.

The color and size of the mane vary between individuals.

AFRICAN
LION

Male lions roar as part of their challenge to other males.

The broad muzzle gives power to the lion's jaws.

HEAD & FACE FACTS

• Cheetahs have longer noses than other cats. This helps them to breathe more easily when holding prey.

• Each individual tiger has distinctive head markings.

• A cat born with four ears was recorded in the US in 1978.

Eyes and ears

As predators, cats depend on their highly developed senses of sight and hearing to find prey. The majority of cats hunt at night, so they need to be able to see in near darkness. A cat can see about six times better than a person can at night. However, a cat's color vision is not as developed as ours. Cats also rely on their acute hearing to pinpoint the exact location of prey. Sounds inaudible to humans, or even dogs, can be detected by cats.

SOUND DETECTORS
The serval, a cat from the African savannah, has large, mobile ears. It can pick up the high-pitched calls of rodents hidden in the grass.

THE OUTER EAR
A cat's outer ear acts like a funnel, channeling sounds to the eardrum. Each ear can rotate to locate sounds precisely.

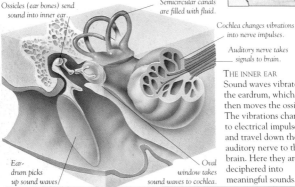

Ossicles (ear bones) send sound into inner ear.

Semicircular canals are filled with fluid.

Cochlea changes vibrations into nerve impulses.

Auditory nerve takes signals to brain.

THE INNER EAR
Sound waves vibrate the eardrum, which then moves the ossicles. The vibrations change to electrical impulses and travel down the auditory nerve to the brain. Here they are deciphered into meaningful sounds.

Ear-drum picks up sound waves.

Oval window takes sound waves to cochlea.

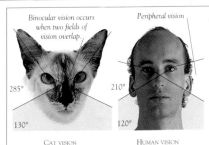

Binocular vision occurs when two fields of vision overlap.

Peripheral vision

285°

130°

CAT VISION

210°

120°

HUMAN VISION

THROUGH A CAT'S EYES
Cats can see at a wider
angle around their heads
than people can. This
allows them to be alert to
movements to the side or
slightly behind them.
Binocular vision allows
them to see images as
three-dimensional, as well
as to judge distance and
depth very accurately.

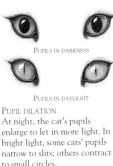

PUPILS IN DARKNESS

PUPILS IN DAYLIGHT

*The mirrorlike
structures in cats' eyes
shine when light reflects
on them at night.*

*In the dark, the pupils
dilate to become
almost round.*

PUPIL DILATION
At night, the cat's pupils
enlarge to let in more light. In
bright light, some cats' pupils
narrow to slits; others contract
to small circles.

SEEING IN THE DARK
Cats see well in semidarkness.
This is because of a "mirror" of
glittering cells (called the
tapetum lucidum) behind
the retina. These cells
reflect light back, making
objects clearer in the dark.

Smell, taste, and touch

Cats have extremely acute senses. They rely on smell to identify the things around them, and on touch to feel their way around, particularly in the dark. Another sensory device cats possess is the Jacobsen's organ, located in the roof of the mouth. This structure seems to respond to both smell and taste, and helps the cat to detect scents that their nose cannot – for example, when a female is ready to mate.

The senses of smell and taste tell the cat if this toad is edible.

Cats never eat anything without carefully sniffing it first.

SENSE OF SMELL

A cat's nose contains some 19 million smelling nerves, compared to a human's 5 million. Cats are especially sensitive to rancid odors, such as meat that has gone off. They normally seek out fresh meat rather than scavenge dead animals.

ENTICING CATNIP

Many cats, especially tomcats, find the smell of catnip irresistible. This garden herb contains a chemical that relaxes cats, or can make them roll around. About 50 percent of cats do not react to catnip at all.

TOUCH-SENSITIVE HAIRS

Whiskers are specialized, stiff hairs with highly sensitive nerves in their roots. They help a cat like this leopard to familiarize itself with its surroundings. A cat uses its whiskers to gauge if it can fit through a gap.

The cat's saliva leaves its scent.

Cats groom each other to spread their scent, and also to show affection.

CAT COMMUNICATION

Cats use smell to communicate far more than people do. They recognize the familiar scents of their companions. Because their skin is covered in touch-sensitive nerves, cats also communicate by grooming each other.

Characteristic lip-curling known as flehmening

FLEHMENING

The curious way that a cat curls its upper lip is called flehmening. It does this to draw smells into the Jacobson's organ in its mouth. Male cats flehmen to detect the scent of nearby females. The Jacobson's organs of the lion and tiger are more sensitive than those of domestic cats.

Paws and claws

A cat uses its paws for everything from gentle grooming to fierce fighting. To aid a cat in one of its most important skills, running, the bones of the feet have evolved so that a cat permanently walks on its toes. In the wild, injuries to the paws can prove fatal, since these can prevent a cat from hunting successfully.

CLAWS FOR CLIMBING

Most cats are masterly climbers, and can make even a vertical ascent with ease. Coming back down is more problematic, since the claws curve the wrong way to grip when descending. Cats awkwardly make their way down a tree backward.

Claws are made of keratin, like human nails.

Dewclaw on front leg is placed like a thumb and helps grip.

Claws dig in to anchor the cat.

Carpal pad on front paw prevents skidding when cat lands.

SPECIALIZED FEET

A cat has furless pads of tough leather on the underside of its paws. These pads enable the animal to stalk silently, and they cushion the impact of landings. Pads also help the cat to "brake" suddenly in mid-run. The cheetah has unique grooved pads to improve its control when running.

SCRATCHING ITS MARK
This jaguar, like other cats, scratches trees to keep its claws clean and sharp. Scratching also marks a cat's territory. A cat leaves behind its scent from glands between its toes, while the scratches themselves show the cat has been in the area.

Claws extended to grasp toy

HUNTING WEAPONS
Watching a cat play will reveal many of its hunting techniques. Cats use their front paws to swipe at, scoop up, rake, or grip their catch. Playing with toys is one way domestic cats practice these moves. Pets tend not to use their claws ferociously against their owners.

This 3-week-old kitten is already beginning to develop its hunting skills.

RETRACTABLE CLAWS
When a cat rests, ligaments keep its claws protected under extensions of the toe bones. The claws are only extended when needed. A cheetah, however, has its claws out permanently so it can grip the ground when it runs.

CLAWS
RETRACTED

CLAWS
EXTENDED

Relaxed cat with claws retracted out of sight

Ligaments slacken to unveil claws when necessary.

FUR TYPES

SLEEK AND FINE, or long and luxurious, a cat's fur is its finest feature. The coat insulates a cat in hot or cold weather, carries its scent, and is sensitive to touch. Fur type is often suited to where a cat lives, although the wide variation of coats in domestic breeds is due to selective breeding by people.

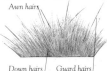

Awn hairs

Down hairs *Guard hairs*

BRITISH SHORTHAIR
This breed is typical of short-coated cats. It has a short, dense, crisp coat. The thick, plush fur stands out from the body like a rug.

Coat is about 2 in (5 cm) thick.

A CAT'S COAT
There are three kinds of hair in a cat's coat, although not every breed has all three. The longest are the coarse outer guard hairs. In wild and domestic cats, these carry the pattern. Slightly shorter awn hairs lie beneath. Short, soft down provides insulation.

PERSIAN
Persian cats have the longest and densest fur of any cat breed. The hairs are silky and fine, giving the cat a very fluffy appearance – even the paws are tufted. In warm summer months the cat molts, which makes its coat look shorter.

Persians have thick down and up to 4-in-long (10-cm) guard hairs.

Fur is especially curly on back and tail.

AMERICAN WIREHAIR

This cat's fur is distinctively wiry and springy. Every hair, including those in the ears and on the tail, is crimped, or even coiled. The Wirehair's fur is of medium length and very frizzy. It feels like lamb's wool to the touch.

Wiry coat makes pattern look raised.

CORNISH REX

The unusual fur of the Rex breeds is wavy and crimped. All of the hairs in a Cornish Rex's coat are short and curly. The coat is made up solely of down and awn hairs, both of which are very soft to the touch. The fur is fine, so Rexes can be susceptible to the cold.

WILD CAT FUR

Wild cats have coats of two layers: warm down hair underneath and a resilient outer coat. In cold climates, cats have thicker fur. Pallas's cat from Asia has the longest coat of any wild cat. It was once mistakenly believed to be the ancestor of domestic cats with long hair.

Longer fur on underside for warmth when lying on cold ground

PALLAS'S CAT

"HAIRLESS" SPHYNX

Although the Sphynx looks bald, it has traces of fur on its tail and a light covering of down on its body. It also has very short eyebrows and whiskers. This breed's lack of hair means that it is vulnerable to sunburn.

Coat is like suede.

Colors and patterns

Cats come in a huge variety of colors and patterns.
Many have distinctive markings that originally
evolved to help cats in the wild stay hidden
from their prey. Domestic cats often come in
more conspicuous colors because they
have little need for camouflage.
Breeders have achieved
some very striking color
and pattern combinations.

SEAL TORTIE
POINT SIAMESE

CORNISH REX
TORTOISESHELL

HIMALAYAN POINTS
Siamese cats have a characteristic pattern of
darker areas on the tail, legs, ears, and face.
These markings are described as points. Young
kittens develop their points as they mature.

*Black and red
randomly but
evenly distributed*

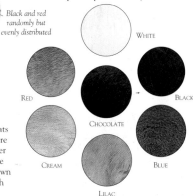

WHITE

RED

BLACK

TORTOISESHELL
For genetic
reasons, tortoiseshell patterns
occur almost entirely in female
cats. Tortoiseshell fur is a
combination of black and red.

CHOCOLATE

COLOR RANGE
Some cats have unpatterned coats
of one pure, solid color. There are
many varieties, some simply paler
versions of the basic colors. Here
the typical darker colors are shown
above their lighter variants, with
white shown on its own.

CREAM

LILAC

BLUE

SILVER SPOTTED
BRITISH SHORTHAIR

Black spots are striking against a silver background.

TABBY MARKINGS

This cat's spotted coat exemplifies the dark markings typical of tabbies. In different tabby cats, the patterning might be stripes, spots, or patches. These patterns are left over from the natural camouflage markings of wild cats. Tabby patterning is very common in feral cats (domestic cats that live in the wild).

WILD CAT PATTERNS

The stripes or spots of a wild cat's coat are vital because they help the animal blend into its surroundings. Patterns camouflage a cat by breaking up the outline of its body shape. The markings of wild cats vary so considerably that the shape of the patterns is one way to distinguish the species. Individual cats of the same species also have slightly varying patterns.

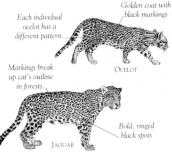

Golden coat with black markings

Each individual ocelot has a different pattern.

OCELOT

Markings break up cat's outline in forests.

Bold, ringed black spots

JAGUAR

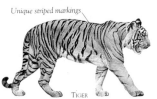

Unique striped markings

TIGER

Named after its cloudlike pattern

Gray-brown coat with marbled markings

CLOUDED LEOPARD

CAT MOVEMENT

NORMALLY GRACEFUL and controlled, cats can also react with a sudden burst of energy. Balance, strength, speed, and quick judgment help cats to chase and seize elusive prey. The only physical quality cats lack is endurance. The cat is a particularly talented leaper, able to jump four and a half times its body length and land on a chosen spot with great accuracy.

JUMPING
Cats can leap vertically when necessary. The caracal and lynx are expert jumpers, leaping up into the air to swipe a bird as it takes off. With one paw, they can knock their catch to the ground.

A kitten extends its paws and claws to prepare for landing.

Head outstretched as cheetah accelerates to its full speed.

CHEETAH

Claws help a cat climb and maintain its balance.

Looking before leaping, to judge its distance from the ground

TERRITORIAL MOVEMENTS
One of a cat's main daily movements is to patrol and mark its territory. It will roam around looking out for other cats or potential prey. Cats climb both to survey their area and because a higher position gives them an advantage over competitors.

LEAPING

A cat's most characteristic movement is its leap, demonstrated here by a lioness. The back muscles flex and relax as the cat leaps, with the tail extended for balance. The powerful back legs lift the cat and are the last part of the body to leave the ground.

The lioness stretches her body forward as she takes off.

Tail is turned up for balance.

Slender, light body and long legs enable the cheetah to reach high speeds.

The tail is more than half the length of the body. It swings to counterbalance the body during sharp turns.

RUNNING

Most cats can leap better than they run, but the cheetah is built for speed. Its backbone is extremely flexible, so when the front legs touch the ground, the back end springs forward. In midstride the body stretches full out and all four legs leave the ground. At full sprint the cheetah can reach 60 mph (96 km/h).

When running, the front paws never touch the ground at the same time as the back paws.

Balancing and falling

Some types of cat spend a significant part of their lives in trees, moving confidently along even the narrowest branches. However, if it does fall, the cat has evolved a unique method of protecting itself. Its eyes, brain, and sensitive balance organs in the inner ear ensure that the cat always lands on its feet.

The head rotates first to align with the ground.

1 INSTANT REACTION
The inner ear instantly reacts if the cat is off balance. This warns the brain that it needs to begin to respond to the fall.

2 ROTATING RAPIDLY
The front of the body receives signals from the brain and twists to follow the head. The backbone is so supple that it can rotate 180°.

Front legs pull around to upright position.

GEOFFROY'S CAT

LIVING THE HIGH LIFE
Many of the small wild cats hunt and sleep in trees. The Geoffroy's cat from South America uses its sharp claws, powerful vision, good reflexes, and superb sense of balance to stalk mammals and birds in the treetops.

This cat lives in the mountainous forests of southern South America.

PERFECT BALANCE
This leopard looks precariously balanced, but it will easily secure its kill off the ground and away from scavengers. The leopard is one of the biggest members of the cat family that spends a lot of time in the trees. It is strong enough to drag up a carcass heavier than its own body weight.

FALLING FACTS

• One cat is known to have survived a record fall of 200 ft (61 m).

• From heights of 60 ft (18 m), cats travel at 40 mph (64 km/h) before they hit the ground.

• If the front legs cannot absorb the force of impact, the cat's chin crashes into the ground. This is likely to cause a jaw fracture.

Back end still recovering

Eyes checking where it will be landing.

The back legs will help to absorb the force of impact.

4 LANDING ON ITS FEET
Only seconds after losing its balance, the cat is well positioned to land safely. The head and soft underparts are protected from injury. The cat instinctively relaxes its body before impact, which prevents it from tearing its muscles or jarring its joints.

3 READY FOR IMPACT
As the cat's front legs begin to stretch out to make contact with the ground, the back of the body is still swiveling around. The collarbones at the top of the front legs will act as shock absorbers when the cat lands.

Legs prepared to run when cat touches ground

Front legs take most of the shock of the landing.

LIFE CYCLE OF CATS

A HEALTHY CAT can live for 10–20 years. Before they are a year old, cats of small species begin to breed. The big cats do not have their first litter until at least the age of three. Female cats have evolved an unusual but efficient breeding cycle. Mating triggers the release of the eggs, increasing the cat's chance of getting pregnant.

LIONS COURTING
A lion grooms his partner before mating. He will try to prevent any other males from coming near. A pair may mate 100 times in a day.

Tom eyes queen.

Finding a partner

Several times a year, when she is ready to mate ("in heat"), a female cat (or queen) calls loudly to reveal her presence. Her urine contains chemical scents known as *pheromones*. These waft through the air, attracting potential mates in the area. She can then select one or more candidates to father her kittens.

1 THE FIRST MEETING
The queen is unlikely to accept a mate immediately. She may even react aggressively at first, before becoming provocative and enticing the tom by rolling on the ground.

Rolling is a typical signal that a queen is in heat.

2 RITUAL REJECTION

The tomcat approaches to make initial contact, but the queen drives off any attempt to mate until she is ready. She will lunge out with her claws or bite to free herself if necessary. He will repeat his advance moments later.

Male tries to grab neck to prevent her attack.

Mating lasts only a few seconds.

Eggs may be released 24 hours after mating.

Female spurns the tom's first approach.

3 MATING

When she is ready to mate, the female raises her hindquarters and puts her tail to one side. The male stops her from turning on him by gripping the loose skin, or scruff, of her neck.

4 AFTER THE ACT

Once they have separated, both cats groom themselves. Cats usually mate repeatedly over a few days. Often the female mates with several toms. As a result, one litter can contain kittens with different fathers.

The male rests for awhile.

The female may not have anything to do with the male after mating.

Growing up

It takes kittens about 65 days to develop in the womb. The pregnancy of big wild cats lasts for 115 days. Once born, all young cats are helpless. They are blind and deaf for over a week and must huddle together for warmth. Kittens grow quickly and are independent by three months, but cubs in the wild can stay with their mother for up to two years.

BEFORE BIRTH
A kitten's organs develop in its first weeks in the uterus. Only in the last three weeks do the fetuses grow much in size. This prevents the mother from being hindered by a weight increase, so she can hunt until late in pregnancy.

Average litter size is four, but some cats have much larger litters.

These kittens are in their last weeks before birth.

Each fetus develops inside a saclike membrane.

FAMILY FACTS
• One Burmese had a record 19 kittens in a single litter.
• All kittens have blue eyes. As they grow up their eyes often change color.
• Cats can breed throughout life; one female had a kitten when she was 28.

FIRST FEEDING
A mother cat must bring up her young on her own. She suckles her kittens for six to eight weeks. Although she has only eight teats, she can rear up to 14 kittens.

The first milk has antibodies to help kittens fight infections.

STARTING ON SOLID FOOD
Young cubs in the wild may not eat meat until
three months old, while kittens are
weaned in about half that time. The
mother still protects her young after
they stop suckling. She also
teaches them cleaning
and hunting skills.

*As the cat grows up, the
color or pattern of its
coat may change slightly.*

*A kitten's fur is
downy soft until it
grows its adult
guard hairs.*

CHEETAH
AND CUBS

A MOTHER'S CARE
Having to look after her cubs alone makes
life difficult for a female cheetah. She is
forced to leave her young while she
hunts, and goes to great lengths to
protect them. From the time they
are born until they are old
enough to follow her, she
may carry them one by one
to up to 20 new
locations. She must
keep them hidden
from predators
like lions and
leopards.

*Nine out of ten
cheetah cubs do
not survive their
first three
months.*

*In its first year, a
young cheetah has
a mane of longer
hair on its neck.*

HUNTING

VIRTUALLY ALL CATS hunt on their
own, so they must attack
with surprise and speed.
They stealthily approach
their unsuspecting prey
using any available cover.
When they are close enough
they suddenly pounce, seizing
their quarry in a deadly grip.

HOUSEHOLD HUNTER
The domestic cat is famed for
its prowess as a mouser. Some cats
also excel at catching lizards, birds,
or insects. However, hunting is a
learned behavior, so not all pet
cats make efficient hunters.

GROUP CHASE
Unlike most cats, lions hunt
in groups. This means they
can kill animals larger than
themselves. The lionesses of
the pride do nearly all of
the hunting. To improve
their chances of a kill,
they single out a weak-
looking animal,
surround it, and then
chase it down.

*Cat holds its body
and tail close to
the ground.*

FATAL BITE
This leopard pins down its victim to stop it from escaping. Then it bites through the neck of its catch to sever the spinal cord. If a cat cannot eat its kill all at once it will drag the carcass under cover to protect it from scavengers.

FRUSTRATED KILLER
Domestic cats will play with a toy as if it were a prey animal. They creep up on the object, then bite and shake it. Wild cats sometimes play with their quarry before killing it.

Spotted coat pattern keeps the animal camouflaged.

Mature cats play occasionally, but not as often as kittens.

ASIAN LEOPARD CAT

SILENT STALKER
Except for the cheetah, cats can manage only short bursts of speed. They must steal quite close to an animal before they bound forward. Approaching slowly and silently, the stalking cat is alert to every movement. When it is within striking distance it springs on its prey without warning.

The cat runs forward in this position, then stops and crouches down.

GROOMING

BOTH WILD AND DOMESTIC cats are extremely clean creatures. Meticulous, regular grooming keeps a cat's coat glossy and healthy by getting rid of dirt, loose hair, and dead skin. Grooming also allows a cat to spread its scent all around its body. Usually grooming is the sign of a relaxed cat, but sometimes it can be a nervous reaction.

WASHING EACH OTHER
A cat may need help cleaning areas it cannot quite reach. Mutual grooming also reinforces the bond between family members, like these kittens, as they spread their scent over each other.

The paws must be kept free of irritating thorns and grit.

Each papilla points backward, so tongue can be used like a rasp.

GROOMING TOOL
The cat's tongue is rough, covered in pointed, abrasive hooks called *papillae*. These enable the tongue to be used like a comb when pulled through fur. *Papillae* are also tough enough to scrape meat off a bone.

Tongue curls like a ladle to lap up liquid.

CLEANING UP
Like domestic cats, wild cats such as this snow leopard often groom themselves when they have finished feeding. This removes the blood from their fur after a kill. Grooming may also help a cat cool off in hot weather as the saliva evaporates from its coat.

Flexible body means the cat can bend to lick almost all areas of its body.

Scent from glands on the chin, paws, and near the genitals is spread all over the coat.

GROOMING FACTS

• Cats always groom themselves after waking from a deep sleep.

• The hair swallowed during grooming can form a hairball in the cat's stomach.

• The largest recorded hairball weighed 2 oz (57 g). It was surgically removed from a 14-year-old cat.

WASHING ROUTINE
Every time it cleans itself, a cat follows exactly the same routine. It licks its paw and wipes it in circles around the sides of the face and the ears.

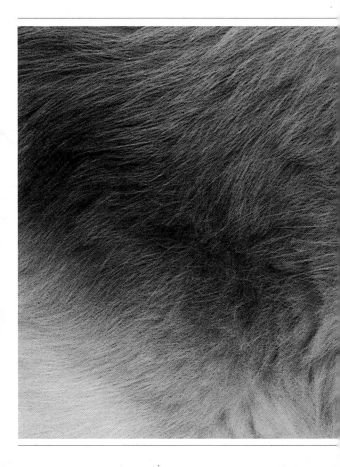

SIMILAR CATS WITH DIFFERENT COATS

ABOUT DIFFERENT COAT LENGTHS

CATS' COATS COME in a wide variety of different lengths and textures. Sometimes these variations have evolved naturally or are the result of chance matings between cats. This section focuses on particular breeds with close relatives that have been purposely bred to achieve a different type of coat.

Distinct ruff of fur around neck

Bushy tail

SILKY TIFFANY
This long-coated counterpart of the Burmese was developed in the 1980s from a desire to create a Burmese with a fluffy coat. The Tiffany is not as popular as its sleek relative. This may be because its long fur conceals the elegant body shape.

BURMESE
A distant descendant of Southeast Asian cats dating back to the 15th century, the Burmese has a fine, short coat, well suited to the heat and humidity of the tropics.

TURN-OF-THE-CENTURY PERSIAN
For the last 100 years, people have
specially bred cats to emphasize
certain features, including coat
length. Comparing this Persian
from the 1900s to its descendant
below shows how, over time,
this breed's coat has become
longer and fluffier.

*Breeders have
enhanced the long,
luxurious coat.*

MODERN PERSIAN
This tortie and white
Persian is a top example
of its kind today. Its
undercoat is so thick
that it makes the
cat appear much
larger than its
actual size.

*Today Persians
come in a huge
range of colors.*

BRITISH SHORTHAIR

PERSIAN

COAT COMPARISON
The length of a cat's coat
does not affect its color.
However, tabby markings
are more distinct on
shorthaired cats because
their hair is compact. In
longhaired cats, the down
hair determines how
dense the coat is.

AMERICAN CURL

THESE UNUSUAL-LOOKING CATS are a recent breed, originating in 1981. American Curls are so-named because their ears curl backward, appearing almost inside out. This chance mutation was noticed by two breeders in California, and has since been developed in both longhaired and shorthaired versions. These cats do not seem to suffer as a result of their curled ears.

LONGHAIRED CURL
The first American Curl was a longhaired female kitten whose ear cartilage began to curve backward a few days after she was born. She passed on this odd trait to two of her kittens.

Silky coat and plumed tail

Cats with curled ears can be bred in any color or pattern.

RED TABBY AND WHITE AMERICAN CURL

Ears can swivel so tips point inward.

Soft, rounded ear tips

CURLED EARS
Instead of rising to a point, the American Curl's ears curve backward to at least a 90° angle. The degree that the ears curl depends on the individual cat.

The base of the ear is quite firm.

Round face with straight nose

TORBIE AND WHITE
AMERICAN CURL

SHORTHAIRED CURL
This fur type was achieved by crossing shorthaired cats with the original longhaired American Curls. It takes four to seven days for a newborn kitten's ears to begin to curl. The ears continue to unfurl for months. Breeders prefer an extreme curl.

Crossing American Curls with Siamese cats has introduced colored points.

SEAL TABBY POINT
AMERICAN CURL

SCOTTISH FOLD

FOLDED OR DROOPY EARS are commonly seen in dogs, but rarely occur in cats. However, in 1951 on a farm near Coupar Angus in Scotland, one kitten in a litter was born with pointed ears that gradually began to turn down toward its face. A local shepherd decided to establish these folded ears in a breed, giving rise to the Scottish Fold.

Small, tightly folded ears lie like little caps on the side of the head.

LONGHAIRED FOLD
Although the original Scottish Folds had short coats, they must have carried a gene for long hair because subsequent litters contained long-coated kittens. Longhaired Folds have thick fur of medium length.

Short, stout legs can sometimes be abnormally thick.

BLUE-CREAM AND WHITE SCOTTISH FOLD

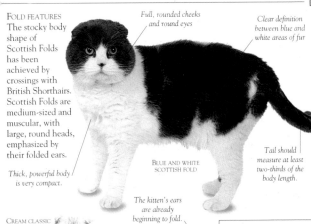

FOLD FEATURES
The stocky body shape of Scottish Folds has been achieved by crossings with British Shorthairs. Scottish Folds are medium-sized and muscular, with large, round heads, emphasized by their folded ears.

Full, rounded cheeks and round eyes

Clear definition between blue and white areas of fur

Thick, powerful body is very compact.

BLUE AND WHITE
SCOTTISH FOLD

Tail should measure at least two-thirds of the body length.

The kitten's ears are already beginning to fold.

CREAM CLASSIC
TABBY KITTENS

SCOTTISH FOLD KITTENS
When first born, all Scottish Fold kittens have normal, pointed ears. After about two or three weeks the tips of the ears begin folding in toward the nose. Folded ears are a dominant mutation, meaning that if only one parent is a Fold, some of the kittens will also show this trait.

Scottish Folds can be bred in a wide variety of colors and patterns.

SCOTTISH FOLD FACTS

• Scottish Folds make placid and friendly pets. They are tolerant of other domestic animals, including dogs.

• The folded shape of these cats' ears does not make them more prone to ear infections than cats with normal ears.

• Scottish Fold cats are always mated to straight-eared littermates, and never to other Scottish Folds, in order to avoid genetic weakness.

ABYSSINIAN AND SOMALI

THE FIRST ABYSSINIAN CAT was brought to Britain in 1868 by soldiers returning from war in Abyssinia (now Ethiopia). Abyssinians look so similar to the cats in ancient Egyptian wall paintings that they are believed to be related. The Somali breed originated from long-coated kittens in Abyssinian litters.

BLUE ABYSSINIAN

RUDDY ABYSSINIAN

Ticked fur is short, thick, and glossy.

TRADITIONAL COLORING
The original Abyssinian is known as the Ruddy, or Usual. It is sometimes called the "rabbit cat" because the orangish brown ticked color of its coat is like a wild rabbit's. These athletic and lively cats have been popular pets for decades.

TWO-TONE COAT
The Blue Abyssinian used to be very rare, but has now become more common. It has a steel blue-gray coat with an oatmeal-colored undercoat. New colors are developed by crossbreeding with other types of cat.

CHOCOLATE
SILVER SOMALI

*Longer fur
on shoulders*

*Dark fur
extends up
back of legs.*

TICKED FUR COLOR

Both Abyssinians and Somalis have what is described as ticked tabby fur. Ticked fur color is caused by light and dark bands that alternate around each hair. The tips of the hairs are always dark. Depending on the width and number of the bands, the coat can be a darker or a lighter shade.

TICKED FUR

LONGHAIRED SOMALI

These cats were named after Somalia, which neighbors Ethiopia, to reflect their similarity to Abyssinians. They differ in the length of fur, but have the same body shape.

SOMALI CHARACTERISTICS

Abyssinians and Somalis can be born in the same litter if the Abyssinian parents carry a longhaired gene. However, Somali parents produce only Somali kittens. It can be 18 months before a kitten's ticking is fully developed.

*Soft, dense fur
does not mat.*

*The base coat is
white with blue
ticking.*

*Full,
bushy
tail*

BLUE SILVER SOMALI

MANX AND CYMRIC

LEGEND CLAIMS THAT 400 years ago, a Spanish galleon wrecked near the Isle of Man, off the coast of England, and tailless cats swam ashore. These were said to be ancestors of the Manx. But the mating of related cats on the island probably resulted in the tailless mutation.

NATIVE CAT
Manx cats are the symbol of the Isle of Man and feature on the island's coins. A cattery has been set up there to breed Manx.

TORTIE AND WHITE MANX

TOTALLY TAILLESS
In the true Manx there is no tail at all, just a hollow at the end of the backbone. This type of Manx is known as a Rumpy.

Shortened vertebrae make back look curved

ORANGE-EYED CYMRIC

Because the front legs are shorter than the back legs, the Manx has an odd, hopping walk.

LONGHAIRED MANX
The Cymric is a rare longhaired form of the Manx. Pronounced *kumric*, its unusual name is Welsh for "Wales." Like the Manx, it has a stocky, muscular body and is long-lived.

JAPANESE BOBTAIL
Shorthair cats with short tails have been known in Asia for 1,000 years. The Japanese Bobtail has a long history in Japan, although it is rare elsewhere. The Japanese believe that cats of this noisy and friendly breed bring good luck. Many Japanese homes are decorated with depictions of Bobtails. Their Japanese name means "beckoning cat" because they are known for raising a paw in greeting.

Pom-pom tail usually kept curled close to body

TORTOISESHELL AND WHITE JAPANESE BOBTAIL

Rabbitlike posture

TORTOISESHELL MANX

Shortened, stubby tail

Massive, muscular flanks

STUMPIES
Manx with short, movable tails are called Stumpies. Longies are Manx with tails of almost the normal length. Tailless Rumpies must breed with Manx with some trace of tail or the kittens are at risk of spinal defects or even death.

PERSIAN AND EXOTIC

LONG-COATED CATS were known in Persia (now Iran) centuries before they were introduced to Europe. This explains how the large, fluffy, flat-faced breed got its name. Exotics have a shorter history. They were developed in the 1960s as shorthaired versions of Persians.

POPULAR VICTORIAN PET
Persians took part in the first modern cat show in 1871 in Britain. Queen Victoria kept Blue Persians, which helped to make this breed very popular during the 19th century both in Britain and in the United States.

Shape of the body is all but hidden by the thick coat.

Short, bushy tail

PERSIAN FEATURES
Breeders have emphasized certain qualities in Persians. The body is massive and stocky, the head is round, and the face extremely compressed. Persians have the longest and densest fur of any cat breed.

In bicolor Persians, white markings cover one-third to one-half of the coat.

CREAM AND
WHITE BICOLOR
PERSIAN

Short, plush coat is easy to care for.

EXOTIC SHORTHAIR
Except for its short, dense coat, the Exotic resembles the Persian in almost every respect. These cats are lively and friendly and come in many colors.

Thick tail with blunt tip

Strong, stubby legs

Small round ears with tufts of fur inside

SHADED GOLDEN EXOTIC

CHOCOLATE PERSIAN

LILAC PERSIAN

COLOR RANGE OF PERSIANS
Persians come in over 30 colors. Their coats can be one pure color, bicolored, or patterned. Persians with pointed markings are called Himalayans in North America.

Broad, muscular chest

NEWLY CREATED COLORS
The Persian's lush coat has been made increasingly glamorous by breeders in search of ever more distinctive colors. The warm, pinkish gray coat of this Lilac is a dilute, or lighter, form of chocolate.

Tufted paws

SIAMESE AND BALINESE

THE SVELTE AND REGAL SIAMESE is one of the best-known cats in the world. This type of cat has been recorded in Thailand (formerly Siam) since the 14th century. The Siamese's longhaired relative, the Balinese, is named after the graceful, swaying dancers of Bali.

Head is triangular, with large ears and almond-shaped eyes.

ANCIENT HISTORY
For centuries, cats with Siamese markings have been painted in Thailand. Legend claims that the first Siamese had crossed eyes from staring at a vase they were given to guard.

SEAL TORTIE POINT SIAMESE

Long, slender body with fine bone structure

Tortoiseshell patterning disrupts the point markings.

POINT PATTERN
Siamese have pale bodies with darker-colored points on the face, legs, feet, and tail. All Siamese kittens are light-colored at birth and develop points over time.

BALINESE

This recent breed is the result of pairings between Siamese and Angoras. Balinese have the same elegant body shape as Siamese cats, but with longer fur and a distinctive plumed tail. They are less vocal than their relatives.

Points occur on parts of the body that have cooler temperatures.

Long, wedge-shaped face

Silky fur grows up to 2 in (5 cm) long.

BLUE LYNX POINT BALINESE

CLOSE RELATION

A popular and friendly breed, the Burmese came about from a mating between a Siamese cat and a brown cat from Burma. Brown cats had been living in Burmese Buddhist temples since the 15th century. Burmese are now bred in many colors.

Slightly stockier body than the Siamese

CHOCOLATE BURMESE

LONGHAIRED CATS

ABOUT LONGHAIRED CATS

APART FROM RARE EXCEPTIONS, wild cats do not have long fur. It would be a disadvantage, getting tangled and caught in undergrowth. However, a few types of domestic cats evolved thick coats. Breeders who desired this trait have since created many longhaired varieties by crossing shorthairs with long-coated cats.

NATURALLY EVOLVED COAT

The Norwegian Forest Cat is an example of a breed that developed long fur for its chilly habitat. A layer of warm down lies underneath the waterproof outer coat.

Pressing on the thick fur leaves an indentation mark.

PRIZE-WINNING LONGHAIR

Cats with long coats were first brought to the West in the 1600s. By the early 1900s, longhaired cats like this one were winning cat shows.

BLUE TORBIE AND WHITE NORWEGIAN FOREST CAT

PRETTY OR PRACTICAL?
Long hair is not just an attractive
feature that has been created
artificially. Dense, long fur is
water-repellent, protecting the cat
from wet and cold weather.
Persians, like the one shown here,
have been bred to possess the
longest coats of any cats. Their fur
can be 4 in (10 cm) long.

SEMILONGHAIR
The Birman's coat is typical of the fur
type known as semilonghair. These
cats have a long, silky top coat and
a very fine undercoat. The Angora
is another example of a
semilonghaired breed.

*Sparse undercoat makes
the Birman's fur
unlikely to mat.*

LILAC POINT BIRMAN

GROOMING A LONGHAIRED CAT
All cats like to keep tidy, but
longhairs need extra help. Daily
grooming is essential if you
own one. Otherwise, not
only will the fur become
matted and soiled, but
you will be faced
with loose hairs all
around the home.
You may also need to
wash the cat.

*Use a bristle
brush.*

*Some cats
enjoy being
groomed.*

Regular grooming prevents knots.

TURKISH ANGORA

ONE OF THE OLDEST longhaired breeds, the Turkish Angora is from Ankara, in Turkey. In the 16th century, Turkish sultans sent these cats as gifts to European nobles. Recently, the breed was saved from extinction by the efforts of the Ankara Zoo.

BLACK TORTIE SMOKE TURKISH ANGORA

Soft, light, silky coat

FATHER OF THE TURKS
This portrait shows the Turkish leader Kemal Atatürk in 1921. Legend held that when he died he would be reincarnated as a deaf white cat, probably referring to an Angora.

NOBLE APPEARANCE
Turkish Angoras have lithe, graceful bodies and long, plumelike tails. Compared to the size of the body, the head is small and angular. These cats have friendly and playful temperaments.

Full, tapering tail

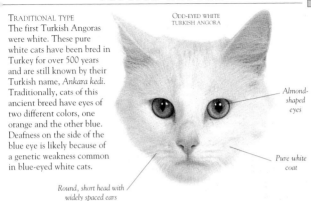

ODD-EYED WHITE
TURKISH ANGORA

TRADITIONAL TYPE
The first Turkish Angoras were white. These pure white cats have been bred in Turkey for over 500 years and are still known by their Turkish name, *Ankara kedi*. Traditionally, cats of this ancient breed have eyes of two different colors, one orange and the other blue. Deafness on the side of the blue eye is likely because of a genetic weakness common in blue-eyed white cats.

Almond-shaped eyes

Pure white coat

Round, short head with widely spaced ears

Long, angular head

Slender, tubular body

ARTIFICIALLY CREATED ANGORAS
In the 1960s, breeders created a new kind of Angora. This breed differs from the Turkish type in that they look like their Oriental ancestors, are more vocal, and have larger litters.

CINNAMON ANGORA

Angoras look more sleek in the summer when they shed their winter coat.

WHITE ANGORA

TURKISH VAN

THE "SWIMMING CAT," or Turkish Van, has been domesticated in Turkey for several centuries, but was unknown elsewhere until 1955. Unlike other long-coated cats, the Turkish Van has no undercoat, so it dries quickly after a swim.

LAKE VAN
Turkish Vans originated in the region of Lake Van in Turkey. The area is stiflingly hot in summer and freezing cold in winter. These cats have adapted to shed most of their winter coat in hot weather.

AUBURN TURKISH VANS

Eyes can be amber, blue, or odd-eyed, with pink rims.

TURKISH VAN PATTERN
These cats have a distinctive chalky-white color with colored areas on the head and tail. The white patch on the center of the head is said by Turkish people to symbolize the thumbprint of the god of Islam.

Turkish Vans are affectionate and lively.

Short, wedge-shaped head with large ears

CREAM TURKISH VAN

SWIMMING CAT
Although most cats hate getting wet, Turkish Vans will swim readily. Their legs propel them forward, while their tail acts like a boat's rudder. Why this behavior evolved is a mystery, but long ago the cats may have been attracted to the fish darting in the shallows of Lake Van.

Feathery, brushlike tail

COVETED CAT
Auburn and cream are the two most common varieties of the Turkish Van. These cats have sturdy bodies and are good climbers. They also have unusual, melodious voices. Since these cats were first brought to the West, this breed has become popular in many countries.

Darker rings may encircle tail, particularly in kittens.

BIRMAN

FROM ITS FABLED PAST in Southeast Asia to its long journey to Europe in the 1900s, the Birman has a colorful history. This ancient breed is known as the sacred cat of Burma because of the mystical legends that surround the origins of its unique white paw markings.

BLUE POINT
BIRMAN

*The kittens'
points will
.darken as
they age.*

DISTINCTIVE PATTERNS
Symmetrical white "gloves"
cover the Birman's front paws.
White fur also extends up their
back legs, like gauntlets.

*Pure white
"gloves"*

BIRMAN BEGINNINGS
In 1919, two travelers brought
the first Birmans to Europe.
Buddhist priests had given the cats to
the couple as thanks for their help in
defending a temple. Only the female cat
survived the tiring trip to the West.
She produced a litter of kittens
soon afterward in France.

BLUE POINT
KITTENS

The Blue Point is one of the traditional colors of this breed.

Medium-length fur is longer on back.

SACRED CAT OF BURMA

The Birman is said to have gained its markings during a battle at a Buddhist temple, like the one above. The story claims that one of the white temple cats touched a dying priest. Its paws remained snow white, its head, tail, and legs became brown, and its back turned golden.

Long body has a strong, stocky build.

ORIGINAL BIRMAN

The Seal Point is the original type of Birman. The fur on its back has a golden glow. Legend claims that during its miraculous transformation the temple cat's eyes changed from yellow to sapphire blue.

SEAL POINT BIRMAN

MAINE COON

THESE CATS were the first long-coated breed to originate in North America. In the 1700s, the Maine Coon's ancestors started to arrive from Europe. These were ships' cats, brought aboard to kill rats. The Maine Coon's odd habit of sleeping in tiny, cramped spaces might relate to its seafaring heritage.

WEATHERPROOFED COAT
The warm, dense coat of the Maine Coon developed to give these cats good protection during the bitter winters of Maine.

Large, solid body

Maine Coons make an unusual chirping sound.

SILVER TABBY
MAINE COON

Sometimes these cats use their front paws to pick up food.

SILVER
TABBY

*Winter
ruff*

RACCOON
This North
American mammal
is often known as
the "coon." Its
markings, long coat,
and striped tail have given rise
to a myth that Maine Coons
descended from raccoons.

WINTER AND SUMMER COATS
The Maine Coon's shaggy coat is
noticeably longer in the winter,
when it has a distinct ruff of fur
around the neck (above). Its thick
coat protects the cat in cold wind
and weather. In the summer, the cat
sheds much of this fur (below).

*Cat grooms long,
bushy tail by
wrapping it around
front leg and
swiveling to lick it.*

*Summer
coat*

BROWN
TABBY

BIGGEST BREED
Maine Coons are some of the
largest domestic cats. They are
very muscular, with powerful
legs and broad chests. This
makes them well suited to
outdoor life. Males are bigger
than females; they may weigh
up to 18 lb (8 kg).

NORWEGIAN AND SIBERIAN FOREST CATS

BOTH THESE WILD-LOOKING BREEDS come from
northern Europe, where the winters are icy cold. This
would explain how their warm, two-layer coats might
have naturally evolved. Another theory suggests that
Norwegian Forest Cats may be distantly related to
Persians or Angoras brought to the
area in the 1500s.

BLUE TORTIE
SMOKE NORWEGIAN
FOREST CAT

RUGGED COAT
Having a double-layered coat helps these
cats stay dry because water runs off the
outer layer of their fur. After a thorough
soaking, Forest Cats are dry in 15 minutes.
If they live indoors or in hot climates,
their fur becomes softer and shorter.

SKILLFUL HUNTER
These intelligent cats
are adventurous
hunters. They
wander widely in
an area, so they
need a lot of room. Forest
Cats are superb, agile
climbers of rocks and trees.

BLACK SMOKE AND
WHITE NORWEGIAN
FOREST CAT

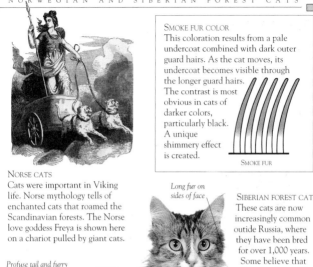

SMOKE FUR COLOR

This coloration results from a pale undercoat combined with dark outer guard hairs. As the cat moves, its undercoat becomes visible through the longer guard hairs. The contrast is most obvious in cats of darker colors, particularly black. A unique shimmery effect is created.

SMOKE FUR

NORSE CATS

Cats were important in Viking life. Norse mythology tells of enchanted cats that roamed the Scandinavian forests. The Norse love goddess Freya is shown here on a chariot pulled by giant cats.

Long fur on sides of face

SIBERIAN FOREST CAT

These cats are now increasingly common outide Russia, where they have been bred for over 1,000 years. Some believe that Siberian Forest Cats were the original longhairs, and all other long-coated breeds are their descendants.

Profuse tail and furry hindquarters

SIBERIAN FOREST CAT

Tabby markings may be the result of matings with wild cats.

RAGDOLL

THESE CATS' STRANGE characteristic of relaxing totally when they are touched fueled the already widespread rumor that Ragdolls feel no pain. This myth first originated when the queen that founded the breed gave birth after being injured in a road accident. However, there is no doubt that Ragdolls are as sensitive to pain as any cat.

BLUE MITTED
RAGDOLL

"Boots" of white
fur on paws

RAGDOLL
KITTEN

ORIGINS OF THE BREED
Ragdolls were developed in the 1960s by a US breeder who wanted to create the perfect house pet. The cats are unusual in that they were bred largely to cultivate their loving temperaments. The Ragdoll was the first breed in history to receive its own trademark.

It takes three years for a young Ragdoll to take on its adult size and color.

YOUNG RAGDOLL
The offspring of Ragdolls are born almost pure white. Their points start to develop after about a week. The shade of the coat varies throughout the cat's life, depending on the time of year. The fur often becomes paler in summer.

Inverted white "V" on face

SEAL BICOLOR RAGDOLL

Odd white spots on colored areas

LUXURIOUS COAT
The silky fur of this breed is medium-length and quite dense. The coat is much longer in the winter, particularly around the neck, where the longer fur looks like a bib. The coat is visibly shorter in summer.

Broad, muscular body

SEAL POINT RAGDOLL

Loose pad of fat on underside

Large, blue eyes

TOLERANT PET
The relaxed nature of these cats gave them their name – they go as limp as a rag doll when they are held. All three varieties of this breed have docile personalities and become totally devoted to their owners.

These cats love children.

IMPOSING SIZE
Ragdolls are one of the largest domestic cat breeds. Mature males can span up to 3 ft (90 cm) when their front and back legs are outstretched. They can reach an average weight of 20 lb (9 kg), while females tend to be lighter – about 15 lb (6.5 kg).

Relaxes completely in owner's arms

NONPEDIGREE

CATS WITH LONG COATS are not always glamorous, purebred show cats. In fact, the humble nonpedigree cat is far more common. There is an infinite variety of longhaired non-pedigree cats. They come in every shape, size, color, and pattern. Each individual cat is totally unique since it has not been specially bred to conform to a set standard.

TABBY MARKINGS
It is more common for nonpedigree cats to have tabby patterns than any other type of markings. This is because tabby is the natural pattern of a cat's coat. In nonpedigree cats, tabby markings are random and individual for every different cat.

Nonpedigree longhairs usually have shorter fur than purebreds.

RED TABBY, OR "GINGER"

STRIKING APPEARANCE

Some nonpedigree cats are distinctive enough to look like show cats. Black-tipped fur gives this cat its silvery shade. Such cats may be used to found new types of pedigree breeds.

TIPPED FUR COLOR

In this type of coat just the tips of the long guard hairs are colored, while the rest of the hair is white. Tipping may occur in the shorter awn hairs as well. The result is a trace of color on the fur, which creates a sparkling effect as the cat moves. Tipping is not commonly seen in non-pedigree cats.

TIPPED FUR

SILVER AND WHITE

POPULAR PET

Nonpedigree cats are far more popular among pet owners than their purebred relatives. They have friendly dispositions and are generally hardy, rarely suffering the health problems that some pedigree cats can be prone to.

WITCH'S FAMILIAR

In medieval times, cats were thought to be linked with witches. This led to thousands of cats being persecuted all over Europe during this period.

Patterning in such nonpedigree cats is entirely random.

Tortoiseshell cats make excellent mothers.

TORTIE AND WHITE

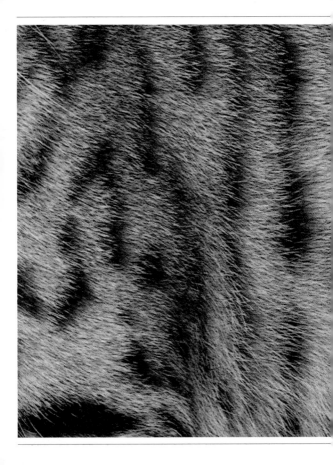

SHORTHAIRED CATS

ABOUT SHORTHAIRED CATS

LIKE THEIR WILD RELATIVES, most domestic cats have short fur. Cats with short coats are popular because they require little grooming, so are easy to look after. Short fur is also genetically dominant; if a long-coated cat mates with a pure shorthair, the kittens will have short coats.

PETS OF THE PAST
Nonpedigree cats with short hair have been popular for centuries. Even today, in spite of the growing number of purebred cats, Nonpedigree cats are still the preferred pets.

SPOTTED MIST
New breeds are constantly being created, whether the crossings are planned or occur by chance. The Spotted Mist is the first breed from Australia. It was developed from crossings based mainly on Burmese and Abyssinians. Their coats are sleek, fine, and delicately spotted.

RED POINT TONKINESE

Blue-green eyes

Short, close-lying fur keeps cat cool in hot climates.

VARIETIES OF SHORTHAIRED COATS

Shorthaired coats can be sleek and fine, like the Siamese, or thick and plush like the British Shorthair. Breeds like the Devon Rex have short, curly fur, while the Manx has a dense, double-layered coat that stands out from its body.

Crossing a Burmese with a Chinchilla Longhair created a soft, dense coat.

BROWN TIPPED BURMILLA

ANCESTOR OF ALL BREEDS

The African wildcat is believed to be the original species from which all of today's domestic breeds evolved. Thousands of years ago, African wildcats were probably attracted to ancient Egyptian settlements, where they fed on mice and rats in grain stores. Eventually some became quite tame.

Coat is soft, with a natural, glossy sheen.

Body shape is a cross between a Siamese and a Burmese.

SHORTHAIRED GROUPS

Pedigree shorthairs fall into three main categories: British, American, or those of Oriental type. The Tonkinese is a member of the latter group. Its soft fur has the same texture as a mink's, so they are often called Minks in the US.

BRITISH SHORTHAIR

THIS STURDY CAT is a popular choice among pedigree
pet owners. Intelligent, friendly, and placid, British
Shorthairs make good
companions. The breed
was developed in the late
1800s from the best of the
nonpedigree cats roaming the
streets of 19th-century Britain.

CREAM AND
WHITE BRITISH
SHORTHAIR

*Short,
strong
legs*

*"M"-shaped
marking on
forehead is
usual in tabbies.*

*This is now the
rarest bicolor
combination.*

STOCKY CAT
A massive, compact body and
a broad, round head are characteristic
of the British Shorthair's body
shape. This shape is described as
cobby. British Shorthairs are larger
than most nonpedigree
varieties. The males in
particular are tough-
looking and muscular,
but they are home-
loving cats with attractive
natures and soft, plush coats.

SILVER SPOTTED
BRITISH SHORTHAIR

*Fur should be
crisp and dense.*

CHOCOLATE
KITTEN

LILAC
KITTEN

COLOR POINTED BRITISH SHORTHAIR

In the 1980s, crossing Himalayans with British Shorthairs gave rise to a cobby breed with points. Friendly and even-tempered, Color Pointed British Shorthairs are calmer than purebred Siamese. They are now being bred in a wide range of colors and patterns.

BLUE POINT BRITISH
SHORTHAIR

Blue
eyes

Coat is short, with
good contrast between points
and body color.

ARRAY OF COLORS

British Shorthairs come in a vast range of colors and patterns. Self (solid) color cats, especially the British Blue, are the most popular. Newer colors, like lilac and chocolate, have recently been created by crossings with Persian Longhairs.

TABBY ORIGINS

Tamed cats with spotted markings date back to ancient Egyptian times. The word "tabby" derives from the old *al Attabiya* quarter of Baghdad, Iraq, where a black and white patterned silk (known in the West as "tabbi") was once made.

Barred tabby
pattern is broken
into spots.

Barring
on legs

Thick tail
with black
tip

SNOWSHOE

WHITE MARKINGS superimposed on a Siamese pattern are the Snowshoe's trademark. This relatively new American breed was not widely known until the 1980s. These cats have active, sunny dispositions, and are gaining popularity in many countries.

SNOWSHOE KITTEN

Bright blue eyes

DISTINCTIVE MARKINGS
Snowshoe kittens are born pure white. Over two years, they develop darker points on the head, legs, and tail, along with the white markings characteristic of the breed. The kitten above already shows the distinctive white paws which earned Snowshoes the nickname "Silver Laces."

Dark points contrast with white markings.

ORIGINS OF THE SNOWSHOE
This breed was founded from three Siamese kittens born with white feet. Some breeders were worried that if these kittens' white markings became established they might spread into Siamese bloodlines. The breed was developed in spite of these concerns, using American Shorthairs to give the Snowshoe a large, strong, muscular build.

SEAL AND WHITE POINT SNOWSHOE

Front paws are white to ankle.

SHOWING CATS
Like other recognized breeds, the
Snowshoe has its own individual
judging standards, although these
may very slightly between different
feline organizations. Cats are judged
on markings, coat condition,
body shape,
and health.

YOUNG
SNOWSHOE

SIZE DIFFERENCE
There is usually a big difference in size
between male and female Snowshoes.
Toms tend to be much larger,
weighing up to 12 lb (5.4 kg).
Males develop prominent
jowls as they mature.

Strong,
muscular
body

Color is
darker in older
cats and in
cold climates.

This young
Snowshoe shows
its Siamese
heritage.

Long tail

White markings on
back legs extend
above the knee.

AMERICAN SHORTHAIR

DESCENDED FROM THE FIRST CATS brought to North America by European settlers in the 1500s, the American Shorthair remains a tough, hardy cat. It is independent and strongly built, a legacy from the frontier cats that lived in the early American settlements. These skilled mousers were not specially bred in their first years, so they evolved along natural lines. Only since the early 1900s have these cats been standardized into a breed.

SHADED SILVER
AMERICAN
SHORTHAIR

Dark shading on back

TYPICAL AMERICAN
Compared to its British counterpart, the American Shorthair is larger and more powerful. It has a less rounded face, a longer nose, and longer legs than a British Shorthair. The fur is very short and coarse, adapted for a harsh outdoor life. This breed normally has a robust and healthy constitution.

Thick fur with hard texture

Longer tail than its British cousin

COLONIAL CATS
For centuries, ships carried cats to kill rats. The cats would disembark at ports around the world, or were brought ashore by settlers anxious to protect grain stores in their new homes.

SHADED FUR COLOR
A coat that is shaded has dark outer guard hairs and a white undercoat. On the guard hairs, the dark shade extends partway down each hair from its tip, but never reaches the root. Shaded coats are darker than tipped, but lighter than smoke fur. The white undercoat is revealed when the cat moves.

SHADED FUR

Bright blue eyes

EXPERT HUNTER
Because it developed largely without human interference, the American Shorthair is well adapted for survival. Its short, square jaws are strong, ideal for catching prey. Having to fend for themselves has given these cats streetwise intelligence.

RED AND WHITE VAN TABBY AMERICAN SHORTHAIR

Long, muscular legs help the cat make high leaps.

AMERICAN WIREHAIR

FRIZZY FUR that looks as if it is standing on end gives the American Wirehair its unique appearance. These uncommon cats originated from a male wiry-haired kitten born in 1967 in Verona, New York. This unusual breed is mostly unknown outside North America.

Tabby pattern looks raised because of wiry fur.

LONDON BOMB SITE
In Britain during World War II, derelict buildings were colonized by feral cats. Wiry-coated cats were first recorded at sites like these. However, they were not bred and soon died out.

SILVER MACKEREL TABBY AMERICAN WIREHAIR

CRIMPED COAT
The American Wirehair's guard hairs are thin and bent at the ends. Every hair is crimped, making the coat springy and dense. The fur feels like lamb's wool to the touch. Wirehair kittens are born with tight, curly coats. It takes four or five months before their fur takes on its adult crimped texture.

Dense fur can be wavy or may even form ringlets.

Round head with prominent cheekbones

Fur under chin and underneath body is less coarse than rest of coat.

Striped pattern is known as "mackerel" because it looks like a fish skeleton.

Hair in ears is also crimped.

ROBUST BREED

American Shorthairs were used to develop Wirehairs, so they share a similar body shape. Wirehairs, like this brown and white tabby, are slightly smaller. These cats are long-lived and have playful and curious natures.

BROWN AND WHITE CLASSIC TABBY

CURLY WHISKERS

Even a Wirehair's whiskers are crimped and curly. If its fur gets wet, it takes several days for it to regain its springiness. The coat requires very little extra attention.

EUROPEAN SHORTHAIR

CATS HAVE LIVED in Europe
for thousands of years, but
the European Shorthair only
became a distinct breed in
1982. Before then, it was
considered identical to the
British Shorthair. There
are only slight differences
between these cats and
their close British cousins.

TORTIE SMOKE
EUROPEAN
SHORTHAIR

ORDINARY ORIGINS
This breed developed from nonpedigree
European cats. Later, these cats were crossed
with British Shorthairs to increase body size.
Now that they are a separate breed, these
crossings are no longer allowed, and European
Shorthairs are evolving along different lines.

EUROPEAN
SHORTHAIR FACTS

• These athletic and
stocky cats make good
pets, but they retain a
strong instinct to hunt.

• There is a rare pure
white form of European
Shorthair with blue
eyes that, unlike most
other blue-eyed white
cats, is not deaf.

*If these cats spend
a lot of time in
strong sunlight, the
black in their
fur can turn a
rusty brown.*

*Compact,
rounded paws*

ANCIENT FRENCH SHORTHAIR
Here at the monastery of La Grande Chartreuse, near Grenoble in France, medieval monks bred the ancient and rare Chartreux breed for its fur. These blue-gray cats are easily mistaken for Blue European Shorthairs because they look so similar. Chartreux cats almost became extinct in the 1920s.

Tabby markings become less distinct during molting.

CREAM SHADED CAMEO TABBY EUROPEAN SHORTHAIR

DISTINCTIVE FEATURES
Today's European Shorthairs have slightly longer heads and sleeker body shapes than British Shorthairs. These cats are bred in many colors and patterns. They are hardy and good-natured, but are currently not as well known as their British and American counterparts.

Thick, short tail

REX BREEDS

UNLIKE ANY OTHER BREED, Rexes have distinctive curly coats. The fur is short and wavy, like the Rex rabbit after which these breeds were named. Crimped coats are a rare but natural mutation, so this kind of fur crops up from time to time in cats in various countries. Today, however, just these three Rex breeds with curly coats are widely kept as pets.

Large ears have rounded tips and are covered with fine fur.

CREAM DEVON REX

The whiskers are crinkly and can be fragile.

Oval-shaped, widely spaced eyes

THE FIRST DEVON REX
Kirlee, the original smoky-gray Devon Rex, appeared in 1960 after a mating between a pet cat and a large, curly-coated cat in the neighborhood. *Kirlee* was born in Devon, a western county of England. Devon Rexes differ from Cornish Rexes in that their fur is more twisted.

PIXIE FACE
The Devon Rex's head is unique. These cats have short, broad faces, large eyes, and prominent cheeks. These features, combined with their large, batlike ears, give them a mischievous appearance, which is in keeping with their playful characters.

MOST RECENT REX
The Selkirk Rex appeared in the US in 1987, and both long- and short-coated forms now exist. The unique texture of the coat is fully developed 10 months after birth. Selkirk kittens shed their first curly coat and have sparse, wiry fur for two to three months before they develop their adult coats.

Both sexes have jowls.

Thick, plush coat with loose curls all over body

BLUE CREAM
SELKIRK REX

CORNISH REX
This breed's coat is exceptionally soft and short since it lacks guard hairs. However, this gives the cat little protection in cold and wet weather. Curly fur and a habit of wagging its tail when contented gives the cat its nickname, "poodle cat."

Rippled fur can be groomed by stroking with the hand.

Siamese-type markings

The coat flattens when wet, only gradually becoming curly as it dries out.

CHOCOLATE
POINT SI-REX
CORNISH REX

Body is thin, but these cats have a tendency to get fat.

SPHYNX

ARGUABLY THE MOST BIZARRE of any cat breed,
controversy surrounds the Sphynx. Some people
believe that the hairless Sphynx
should no longer be bred, as its
lack of fur may be bad for the
cat's health. Hairlessness can
occur naturally in animals like dogs
and mice, but it is a very rare trait.

BLACK AND
WHITE SPHYNX

Skin has a
suedelike
texture.

SPHYNX FACTS

• Lack of fur leaves
these cats vulnerable to
cold and sunburn.

• The Sphynx often
rests with one paw held
off the ground.

• The Sphynx is warm
to the touch, hence its
nickname, "suede hot
water bottle."

BALD BODY
Modern Sphynxes
originated from a mutant
kitten born to a black and
white cat in Canada in 1966.
The color of a Sphynx comes
from pigmentation in its skin.
The pink areas correspond to
what would be white fur in a
cat with a coat, and the dark
skin with what would be dark fur.

BROWN AND
WHITE SPHYNX

WORRIED BROW
The Sphynx has an angular face, with
wrinkled skin on the forehead. The ears are
very large and triangular, with rounded tips.
The whiskers are either short and stunted
or they may be completely absent.

*Eye
color
should
complement
skin color.*

*Pronounced
cheek bones*

BROWN AND
WHITE SPHYNX
KITTEN

BORN FURRY
A young Sphynx is born with
a light covering of fur. This is
gradually lost as it grows older,
leaving the body entirely hairless
except for the tail, face, ears, and
feet. The kitten's loose and
wrinkly skin will become
smoother with age.

*Barrel-shaped
chest*

*Each cat has a
unique pattern.*

*Tuft of hair on
tip of tail*

*Sphynxes are unusual
in that they sweat, so
they need to be cleaned
with a damp sponge.*

AZTEC CAT
HEAD
SCULPTURE

AZTEC ORIGINS
Hairless cats were first bred by the
Aztecs, who lived in Mexico in the
14–15th centuries. This sculpture is
thought to be a portrayal of a domestic
cat from the Aztec era. They also
developed a hairless dog breed that still
exists, but the early hairless cats are extinct.

CALIFORNIA SPANGLED

UNIQUELY LAUNCHED in the 1986 Christmas catalog of Neiman-Marcus, this breed created a stir from the start. In keeping with its wild appearance, the California Spangled is intelligent and active. Interest in these cats is so great that there is a long waiting list for Spangled kittens.

ENVIRONMENTAL SYMBOL
The idea behind the breeding of the California Spangled was to raise concern among cat-lovers about the plight of the world's wild cats. Hence, these cats' lean, muscular bodies and striking spotted coats are reminiscent of wild cats.

Spots can be round, square, or triangular.

GOLD CALIFORNIA
SPANGLED

Paul Casey holding Yuma, an 8-month-old Silver

INSPIRATION FOR THE BREED
A leopard he saw on a visit to Africa inspired Paul Casey to create the California Spangled. He hoped to spur people into acting to protect endangered wild cats, but only domestic cats were used to develop this breed. It took six generations to achieve the features he desired.

PURPOSEFUL BREEDER
In 1971, Paul Casey, a scriptwriter from California, began his quest to develop a wild-looking breed. He named the first cats after Native American tribes.

Rounded ears set back on head, away from face

SPANGLED COAT
The patterned coat of this breed is paramount. Each variety has nearly identical markings, differing only in color. The one exception is the "Snow Leopard," which is born pure white and develops spots gradually.

BLUE CALIFORNIA SPANGLED

EGYPTIAN MAU

THIS RARE BREED claims a lineage stretching back thousands of years to ancient Egypt. The markings of the Egyptian Mau are similar to those of cats depicted on Egyptian scrolls and tomb paintings. The modern Egyptian Mau originated in the 1950s from a spotted cat brought to Italy from Cairo, Egypt by a princess.

ANCIENT
EGYPTIAN CAT
SCULPTURE
(600 B.C.)

SILVER
EGYPTIAN MAU
KITTEN

*Mau kittens have
less distinct
markings than
adults*

*Rounded face
and large,
pointed ears*

BLACK SMOKE
KITTEN

SACRED CAT
The ancient
Egyptians
believed cats
were divine. They worshiped
the cat goddess, Bastet, among
other deities, and made
sculptures and other artifacts
in her honor. Killing a cat
was punishable by death.

NOBLE BACKGROUND
"Mau" was the ancient
Egyptian word for the sacred
domestic cat. Today's breed
was developed mainly in
the US. These cats
come in three traditional
colors – silver, bronze, and the
darker black smoke.

ATTRACTIVE EYES

One of the most appealing features of Egyptian Maus are their unusual green eyes. This color takes up to two years to develop fully, and may turn a paler green as the cats age. The eyes are oval and very large. Their slanted shape is emphasized by dark lines running across the cat's cheeks.

SILVER
EGYPTIAN
MAU

Characteristic "M"-shaped tabby marking in center of head

"Mascara lines" on face are reminiscent of ancient Egyptian face makeup.

ORIENTAL SPOTTED TABBY

The Oriental Spotted cat was once called an Egyptian Mau even though it is a separate breed. Now classed as an Oriental Shorthair, this type of tabby developed from Siamese cats and has no connection with Egypt.

Spots are round and evenly distributed on the body.

Dark stripe runs down the back, breaking into bands on the tail.

OCICAT

ONE OF THE NEWER shorthaired breeds, the wild-looking Ocicat emerged in the US in 1964. The breed came about from an unplanned mating between a Siamese and an Abyssinian–Siamese cross. The name "Ocicat" was derived from a combination of the breed's two previous names: "Accicat," reflecting its accidental origins, and "Ocelette" because of its resemblance to an ocelot.

CHOCOLATE OCICAT

Almond-shaped eyes

Large, strong body

Muscular legs with dark markings

Powerful, oval-shaped paws

CUBLIKE KITTENS
Young Ocicats are born with delightful spotted patterning, although their markings are less distinct than those of adult Ocicats. The kittens' coats begin to change about five weeks after birth. The first Ocicat kitten's resemblance to a wild cub so enchanted the original owner that she went on to found the breed.

Glossy, fine, short fur is ticked with at least two bands of color.

SILVER OCICAT

Black line encircles brick-red nose.

DISTINCTIVE COAT
Dark lines extend around the neck and legs. The rest of the body is covered in spots about the size of thumbprints. Each cat's pattern is individual.

Long, patterned tail ends in a black tip.

Dark markings are clear on lighter background.

WILD OCELOT
The Ocicat's markings are said to look like those of this small wild cat, which ranges from the southern US southward as far as Argentina. In some areas, they have been heavily hunted for their beautiful fur.

Unlike other cats, ocelots may live in pairs.

OCELOT

The markings are highly individual.

OCICAT FEATURES
The body shape of the Ocicat is partway between the svelte Oriental and the sturdy American Shorthair. The breed's large, well-muscled body gives an impression of power and strength.
Ocicats are friendly and have a reputation for doglike loyalty to their owners.

ORIENTAL SHORTHAIR

LITHE AND ELEGANT, this breed is a successful attempt at creating Siamese cats without pointed markings. Oriental Shorthairs are intelligent and lively and come in a huge range of colors and patterns. These stylish cats are steadily growing in popularity.

CHOCOLATE
CLASSIC TABBY
ORIENTAL
SHORTHAIR

Oysterlike marking on flank is a feature of all classic tabbies.

Bracelets of chocolate-brown fur on legs

Long, svelte body with sleek fur

Delicate, oval paws

Long, slender legs

ORIENTAL SHORTHAIR FACTS

• Almost every variety of Oriental Shorthair has green eyes.

• These cats are quieter than Siamese cats, but are just as demanding.

• In 1951, the first Oriental Shorthair (a Havana Brown) was created by breeders.

SVELTE SHAPE
Like the Siamese, this breed has a thin, almost tubular, body shape. Slender legs and a long, narrow tail add to their sleek elegance. Orientals are exceedingly agile; they can jump, run, and climb with graceful ease.

HUGE VARIETY
In recent years, the number of different types of Oriental Shorthair has expanded greatly. Using the myriad colors and patterns already available, it is estimated that 400 varieties could ultimately be created.

BLACK ORIENTAL OR EBONY
The Ebony is one of the original Oriental varieties. It arose from crosses between Siamese cats and Russian Blues, and has silky, jet-black fur. Like other Orientals, it is active and energetic and can be trained to walk on a leash.

Angular head with large, pointed ears

CHOCOLATE
TORTIE
ORIENTAL
SHORTHAIR

RED ORIENTAL
Solid (or "self") colored types of this breed were formerly known as Foreign Shorthairs, but now this description is used just for the Foreign White. The Oriental Shorthair grouping today also includes patterned varieties such as tortoiseshells and tabbies.

Random, mottled pattern

Close-lying fur is short, fine, and glossy.

KORAT

PRIZED IN ITS NATIVE SIAM (now called Thailand) for centuries, the Korat is one of the most ancient of all cat breeds. These dusky blue-silver cats have a regal and well-recorded history in Southeast Asia. The Thai people call the Korat "Si-sawat" because of its reputation for bringing its owners good fortune and happiness.

KING RAMA V
It is said that Rama V, king of Siam from 1873 to 1910, named the Korat after the Thai province where these attractive cats have been kept for centuries.

KORAT

Fine, silky fur lies close to the body.

LUSTROUS COAT
A Korat's fur is a lush blue tipped with silver. This gives the coat a silvery sheen. These cats lack a warm undercoat because of their tropical origins, and must be protected from getting chilled.

ANCIENT HISTORY
Korats are lovingly and poetically described in the Southeast Asian *Cat Book Poems*, written between 1350 and 1767. One ancient Thai legend claims that the breed was originally developed by two hermits.

Medium-sized, lithe, and muscular body

104

LUCKY WEDDING GIFTS
Because Korats are considered
symbols of good luck in Thailand,
they are popular gifts for
newlywed couples. It is claimed
that in the past Korats were used
in rain-making ceremonies.
These sweet-natured, home-
loving cats have also gained
many followers since their
introduction to the West in
the late 1950s.

Traditional Thai bride and groom

THAI WEDDING CEREMONY

KORATS

Round, luminous green eyes and distinctive heart-shaped face

Korats have affectionate and playful temperaments.

RUSSIAN SHORTHAIR

THIS NOBLE BREED has a singularly soft, plush coat. The Russian Shorthair evolved near the Arctic Circle, farther north than any other breed. Mystery surrounds its origins, though there is much evidence that it is a native Russian cat. Originally, all Russian Shorthairs were blue, but today new colors are being developed.

RUSSIAN
BLUE

FAMOUS RUSSIAN

The most famous Russian Blue was the pampered pet of Czar Nicholas I, emperor of Russia (1825-55). Although these cats are considered portents of good luck in Russia, the breed has become rare in its native land.

Evenly blue-colored fur tipped with a silvery sheen

UNIQUE CHARACTERISTICS

The double-layered coat of the Russian Shorthair is one of a kind. It is so dense and plush that the hair stands out from the body, like seal fur. The body is long, graceful, and strong. Docile and quiet, these cats are popular pets, particularly in Sweden and New Zealand.

Emerald-green eyes

ARCHANGEL CATS

Russian Shorthairs traveled on ships sailing from the Russian port of Archangel (above) at least as long ago as the 1800s. This gave them their original name, Archangel Cats. For unknown reasons, this breed has also been known as the Spanish Cat and the Maltese Cat.

NEW COLORS

The traditional Russian Shorthair is blue, a color that still predominates today. Recently, breeders in Australia and New Zealand have developed pure white and pure black varieties, which are becoming more popular.

RUSSIAN WHITE

Large, upright ears of thin skin

Delicately boned legs with small paws

White fur appears almost translucent.

SINGAPURA

THIS TINY BREED is a newcomer to the West, although it originated from the feral "drain cats of Singapore" that have lived in the streets of that Asian island for centuries. Developed in the US in 1975, Singapuras are quite scarce, and their rarity means that they can fetch a very high price.

Eye color changes at nine weeks.

SINGAPURA KITTENS

Eyes and nose are outlined in black.

TICKED FUR
Singapura fur is a warm ivory color, ticked with dark seal brown. The tips of the hair are dark.

Sleek and silky fur feels like satin.

SINGAPURA FACTS

• This breed's name is Malaysian for the island of Singapore.

• The feral ancestors of this breed are known for taking shelter in the drains of city streets.

• In 1988, an owner was offered $10,000 for his adult male Singapura.

SMALLEST CAT
This breed is the smallest in the world. A Singapura male often weighs under 6 lb (2.7 kg), compared to one of the largest cats, the Maine Coon, which weighs in at 18 lb (8 kg).

Large eyes and ears in proportion to the small head

FERAL CATS OF SOUTHEAST ASIA
Untamed cats living in the countries of
Southeast Asia have been used in recent years
to create other new breeds, such as the
Ceylonese and the Wild Abyssinian. The feral
cats shown above are from Indonesia, which
has one of the world's largest cat populations.

SINGAPURA CHARACTERISTICS
The small, delicate body of this cat is
emphasized by its fine, close-lying coat.
Its ticked fur is described as "agouti"
because of its resemblance to the
South American rodent of that
name. These cats can be quite
bold. They enjoy the company
of people and often have
inquisitive natures.

SINGAPURA

Underparts are paler than sides of body.

Tail is darker brown than rest of body.

BOMBAY

JET-BLACK FUR that shines like polished patent leather and vivid gold or copper eyes set the Bombay apart. The breed arose in 1958 when a pure black American Shorthair and a sable Burmese were crossed with the aim of creating a cat that looked similar to a miniature black panther.

BOMBAY

Wedge face with short muzzle

Eyes are blue at birth, then turn gray before finally changing to copper or gold.

BOMBAY MARKET
This breed is named after the busy, colorful city of Bombay. This city is the cat's namesake because it is located in India, where black panthers are found.

OUTGOING PERSONALITY
An incredibly affectionate breed, the Bombay makes an ideal family pet. It has an assertive nature and is not easily intimidated by dogs. These cats are also vocal and virtually never stop purring. Bombays crave attention and hate to be left alone.

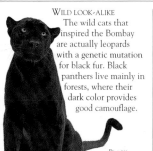

WILD LOOK-ALIKE
The wild cats that inspired the Bombay are actually leopards with a genetic mutation for black fur. Black panthers live mainly in forests, where their dark color provides good camouflage.

BLACK PANTHER

SELF FUR COLOR
The Bombay is an example of a self, or solid, colored cat. This means that the fur is a single color from root to tip. The depth of color along the length of each individual hair does not vary. Typical self colors are black, white, red, and chocolate, or lighter shades of these, like blue, cream, and lilac.

SELF FUR

All Bombays are black – there are no other color varieties.

Gleaming fur is short and dense.

Medium-sized body is firm and muscular.

Medium-length tail

DOMESTIC HYBRIDS

INTEREST IN TRANSFERRING the markings of wild cats to domestic bloodlines has led to the creation of new breeds. The appearance of these hybrids is strongly influenced by their wild cat parent.

Strong, rounded head shape

SERVAL
These tall African wild cats are less fearful of people than some of their relatives. Their attractive spotted markings provided the inspiration for the Savannah breed.

SAVANNAH

Large, round ears

Tabby barring on the legs

SAVANNAH
The Savannah resulted from crosses between servals and domestic cats in the US during the 1990s. The first generation (F1) offspring were very shy, but subsequent matings restricted to domestic cats have produced offspring much closer in temperament to other breeds.

BENGAL CAT

The product of matings involving the Asiatic leopard cat, the Bengal was originally created as part of a genetic research program in the 1960s, but it has now become very popular with cat lovers worldwide. Its coat is dense and luxurious, as well as attractively patterned. Pale-coated individuals are described as Snow Leopards.

Long, powerful tail

Necklaces of black fur on the throat

WILD ABYSSINIAN

Legs have tabby barring

WILD ABYSSINIAN

In spite of its name, this ticked tabby breed was created from feral cats in Singapore during the 1980s. Unlike the Bengal and Savannah breeds, it has never become common.

Large, rosette-like spots on the body

BENGAL

HYBRID FACTS

• Savannahs are the tallest of all cat breeds, standing up to 2 ft (61 cm) at the shoulder.

• The Chausie is another hybrid breed being developed in the US. Its wild ancestor is the jungle cat.

• Infertility among the first male hybrids is a common problem.

NONPEDIGREE

THE POPULARITY of these cats has been unchallenged since their domestication 5,000 years ago. Today, over 95 percent of the world's feline pets are nonpedigrees. These adaptable cats are as diverse as they are numerous. Each one has a unique appearance and personality.

Nonpedigree cats have highly individual markings.

BROWN TABBY

COMMON CATS
In many parts of the world, cats have featured in literature and art through the ages. One example is the famous Cheshire cat from Lewis Carroll's *Alice's Adventures in Wonderland* (1865). The grinning cat completely disappears except for his smile.

HUGE VARIETY
Most nonpedigree cats have tabby markings, a legacy from their wild relatives. Bicolored mixes are also common. Nonpedigree cats with coats of one pure color are much rarer.

ROBUST CITY PETS
Ordinary nonpedigrees are the most commonly kept cats in the world, partly because they are hardy and easy to care for. Black and white cats make ideal city pets because they have unshakable temperaments.

White hairs intermingled with black

White patches are random.

Sturdy body shape

BLACK AND WHITE

Small, widely spaced ears

Nonpedigree tomcats often have prominent jowls.

Broad tail with rounded tip has tabby markings along its length.

TERRITORIAL TOMS
Both male and female cats patrol their territories, but tomcats lay claim to a much wider area. Male cats mark their part of the neighborhood by spraying urine, leaving scratch marks, or rubbing their scent onto objects. They will fight to protect their territory.

Muscular, compact body

RED AND WHITE TABBY

The gene for red fur is likely to have originated in Asia.

Short legs, ending in powerful paws

NONPEDIGREE FACTS
• The lifespan of a nonpedigree cat is normally longer than that of a purebred cat.

• The oldest recorded domestic cat, a Sphynx, lived to the age of 34 years, 2 months.

• A cat's coat color seems to reflect its temperament. In general, tabbies are placid and calm.

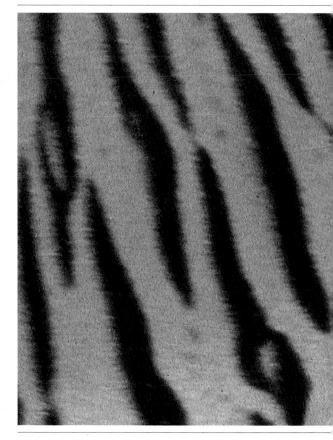

THE WORLD'S WILD CATS

ABOUT WILD CATS

THESE SHY AND MAINLY SOLITARY animals are highly sophisticated hunters. Most use the darkness of night to conceal themselves as they stalk their prey. Wild cats have been resilient and adaptable, successfully exploiting most of the world's habitats. However, many of these graceful creatures have become endangered because of hunting and habitat destruction.

SOFT AND STRIKING FUR
The ocelot is found in forests and scrubland from the southwestern US to the tip of South America. However, today it is quite rare. Like many other strikingly patterned cats, it has been heavily hunted for its beautiful fur coat.

The ocelot stands about 18 in (45 cm) at the shoulder.

OCELOT

WILD CATS' HABITATS
The world's cats have adapted to live wherever they can find prey, from scorching deserts to icy uplands. This Siberian tiger from central Asia hunts throughout the winter. The largest of cats, it roams over a vast area in search of prey.

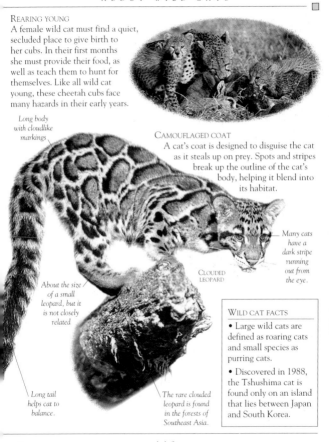

REARING YOUNG
A female wild cat must find a quiet,
secluded place to give birth to
her cubs. In their first months
she must provide their food, as
well as teach them to hunt for
themselves. Like all wild cat
young, these cheetah cubs face
many hazards in their early years.

*Long body
with cloudlike
markings*

CAMOUFLAGED COAT
A cat's coat is designed to disguise the cat
as it steals up on prey. Spots and stripes
break up the outline of the cat's
body, helping it blend into
its habitat.

*Many cats
have a
dark stripe
running
out from
the eye.*

CLOUDED
LEOPARD

*About the size
of a small
leopard, but it
is not closely
related*

*Long tail
helps cat to
balance.*

*The rare clouded
leopard is found
in the forests of
Southeast Asia.*

WILD CAT FACTS
• Large wild cats are
defined as roaring cats
and small species as
purring cats.
• Discovered in 1988,
the Tshushima cat is
found only on an island
that lies between Japan
and South Korea.

SMALL WILD CATS

THE SMALL WILD CATS are less well known than their larger relatives, but are far more numerous. The 28 species range from the tiny black-footed cat of southern Africa to the large puma. Many live in forests, where their striking, spotted patterns help them blend into the dappled shade.

ASIAN
GOLDEN CAT

*Golden cats
have been
known to be
tamed.*

ASIAN GOLDEN CAT

These cats are found in tropical forests of Nepal and Southeast Asia. Like most small cats, they are expert climbers and can catch birds in the treetops. Shy and elusive, Asian golden cats are rarely seen in the wild. They have become scarce since their habitat is destroyed by logging and farming.

FISHING CAT

These unusual Asian cats live close to water, where they grab fish, clams, snails, and other water-dwelling creatures from the shallows. Their front toes are webbed, which enables them to scoop prey out of the water. Their webbed paws also help them swim to hunt for fish.

THE WILDCAT
Varieties of the wildcat are found in Africa, Asia, and Europe. This Scottish wildcat may look like a domestic tabby, but it is a fierce hunter of rodents and birds. Wildcats in Europe generally live only in very remote areas. The African wildcat, the ancestor of all today's domestic breeds, is not as shy and can be found living close to human settlements.

Geoffroy's cat is about the same size as a domestic cat.

SAND CAT
Dense mats of fur protect these cats' feet from the searing hot Saharan sand. They will burrow underground, then wait until nightfall to emerge to hunt.

The sand cat weighs only 5 lb (2.3 kg).

GEOFFROY'S CAT
This high-altitude species is known in the southern part of South America where it lives as "the mountain cat." It has a short, broad head and can run, swim, and climb with ease. Geoffroy's cat may sleep in holes in trees during the day.

Fur keeps cat warm and provides camouflage.

SERVAL AND CARACAL

THE GRASSLANDS and semideserts of Africa are home to these two medium-sized species. The caracal also ranges across the Middle East and Asia. Servals and caracals are formidable hunters, using their large ears to pinpoint small animals foraging in the grass.

SERVAL

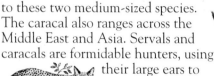

SERVALS AND PEOPLE
Servals have long been hunted in Africa for food or for their skins, which are made into fur cloaks called *karrosses*. In East Africa, these cats are also sometimes kept as pets.

Each cat's pattern is different.

Pure black servals sometimes occur, particularly in Kenya.

SAVANNAH CAT
The serval stands about 24 in (61 cm) tall at the shoulder. It lives alone, usually near water, and employs its superb hearing and vision to track down its prey, often at dusk.

Like other small cats, servals cannot roar, but they do purr occasionally.

Very long front legs help these cats make quick escapes from hunting dogs.

Short tail

DESERT DEN
Open, arid country is the caracal's hunting ground. This cat is sometimes called the desert lynx, although it does not live in true deserts, nor is it a lynx. The female caracal makes her den in burrows or rocky caves, where she gives birth to up to four young. Caracals are now quite scarce.

NOCTURNAL HUNTER
Although caracals can kill animals much larger than themselves, they normally eat lizards, birds, small mammals, and even insects. They are very stealthy, keeping quiet so they can hear tiny movements as they stalk after nightfall.

The name comes from the Turkish "karakal," which means "black ears."

Fur tufts on ears can be 1.75 in (4.5 cm) long.

CARACAL

INDIAN PAINTING OF A CARACAL AND TRAINER

Caracal in bird-catching competition

TRAINED BIRD CATCHER
The caracal is known for its prowess at catching birds. It uses its paws to knock the birds to the ground as they take flight. For centuries, people in India have trained caracals for this skill.

Caracals can make a barking noise.

CHEETAH

THE SWIFTEST MAMMAL in the world, the cheetah outshines all other hunters when it comes to chasing down fast prey. These cats were once trained as hunting animals.

CHEETAH

During the 1600s, the Mogul emperor in India kept 1,000 cheetahs. His collection included a very rare white cheetah with bluish spots.

DANGEROUS DECLINE
Cheetahs almost became extinct during the last ice age. Only a tiny number survived. Since then, inbreeding over generations has caused a serious decline in the fertility of some males. Cheetahs are further threatened by poachers.

Flexible back

Long, slender legs

WATCHFUL MOTHER
The female cheetah is solitary, looking after her two to four cubs on her own. She will feed and protectively guard her young until they are 15 months old.

KING CHEETAH

Lives mainly in southern Africa

Dark markings form stripes instead of spots.

These sleek cats live in the grasslands of Africa.

Skull is small, but longer than in other cats.

Distinctive lines run down face from the eyes.

Golden coat with black spots camouflages the cat as it hunts during the day.

Claws extended permanently to dig in when running

CHEETAH

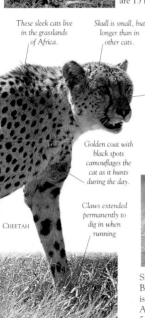

RARE STRIPED MARKINGS
A cheetah with this unusual and very rare coat pattern was first reported in 1927. Although once mistakenly thought to be a separate species, the king cheetah occurs in litters along with normal, spotted cheetahs.

SPRINTING CAT
Because it specializes in running, the cheetah is placed in a different genus from other cats. A cheetah can reach a maximum speed of 54 mph (87 km/h) over a short distance.

JAGUAR AND LEOPARD

THESE TWO BOLDLY MARKED cats are often mistaken for each other. Leopards live in Africa and Asia, and they are agile, expert climbers. Jaguars are American cats with large, stocky bodies. They swim much better than they climb.

JAGUAR

Large, ringed spots shaped like rosettes

SOUTH AMERICAN CAT
Jaguars now live mainly in the tropical forests of Central and South America. They are the largest cats on the American continents and were respected and admired by the Aztecs and Incas.

DARK CAMOUFLAGE
The black panther is simply a black-colored leopard that lives in the dense, shadowy forests of Asia. It shares all the characteristics of its spotted counterpart.

Faint spotted pattern is visible on coat.

BLACK PANTHER

KILLED FOR THEIR FUR
Although trade in jaguar skins is illegal, these pelts are proof that hunting continues. Hundreds of jaguars and leopards have been killed in recent years.

SWIMMING HUNTER
Jaguars swim well and often hunt in water, catching turtles, caimans, and fish. When the river level is low, these cats may even swim out to exposed sand banks and dig up turtles' nests for the eggs.

Perfectly balanced when climbing or resting

LEOPARD

There may be as many as 700,000 leopards in Africa.

LOUNGING LEOPARD
These superb climbers laze around in trees after they have consumed their kill. Here they are safe and can survey their surroundings. Leopards in national parks tend to be much less wary than their unprotected kin.

Powerful paws help the leopard catch large prey like young giraffes.

PUMA, LYNX, AND BOBCAT

EQUALLY AT HOME on rocky mountain slopes or in semidesert scrubland, these three adaptable cats can cope with hot, dry summers as well as cold, snowy winters. The puma and bobcat are found only in the Americas, while the lynx ranges over North America, Europe, and Asia. The closely related lynx and bobcat are distinguished from other cats by their unusual short, stumpy tails.

BOBCAT

The bobcat is one of the most common American wild cats.

Long side whiskers

Long legs

MOUNTAIN HUNTER
Pumas have strength and stamina. These cats will search huge distances for their prey. They may drag their catch 1,300 ft (400 m) from the site of the kill, to hide the carcass from scavengers.

NORTH AMERICAN CAT
The bobcat's range stretches from Canada to Mexico. It is smaller than the lynx and its fur is more coarse, so its pelt is not considered as valuable. The bobcat occasionally strays into the suburbs of cities to catch rats and other small prey.

Sandy brown coat is perfect for high plains camouflage.

ENDANGERED EUROPEAN

The Spanish lynx is much smaller than the Eurasian lynx. It usually hunts rabbits, birds, and fish, but can also take young deer. These cats are extremely endangered – southern Spain is their last major stronghold.

Heavily spotted coat

SPANISH LYNX

TRAPPING FOR FUR

In winter, a lynx's coat is soft and thick, making these cats long sought after by trappers. Today, trapping is regulated. The North American lynx population varies mainly with the rise and fall in the number of its main prey, the snowshoe hare.

PURRING PUMA

The puma (its name is derived from an Inca word) is also known as the cougar or mountain lion. It is now found mainly in South America and the western US. Florida also has a tiny population. Traffic accidents are the major hazard for the 20–50 pumas left in Florida.

The pupils are round, like those of the larger cats.

PUMA

LION

THESE MAJESTIC CATS once roamed from the southern tip of Africa to the Mediterranean and east through Asia. The Romans used to capture lions to fight gladiators in their arenas. Since then, the lions' range has dwindled to scattered areas of Africa and a small forest in India.

FEARSOME KILLER
Although lions rarely prey on people, this panel from the 8th century B.C. shows that it sometimes occurs. In recent times, lions killed 30 workers during the building of a railway in East Africa.

PROUD PAIR
Lions live in open country. The females do most of the hunting, cooperating to chase down prey. The male's job is to defend the pride's territory from other lions. His tremendous roar can be heard up to 5 miles (8 km) away.

FAMILY LIFE
Lions are the only cats that live in groups. The pride may have about 12 members, most of them related females and their cubs. When the young males reach adulthood they must either leave or fight the dominant male.

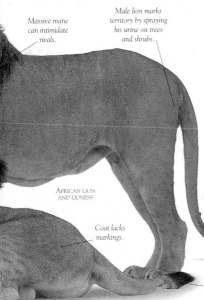

Massive mane can intimidate rivals.

Male lion marks territory by spraying his urine on trees and shrubs.

AFRICAN LION AND LIONESS

Coat lacks markings.

ASIATIC LIONS
At the beginning of the century, there were less than a dozen lions left in Asia. Today, under strict protection in the Gir Forest of India, their numbers have risen to about 300.

Tail, especially the tuft, is used to communicate with other lions.

TIGER

THIS LARGEST MEMBER of the cat family is potentially the most ferocious. The tiger must claim a large territory in order to catch the food it needs to survive. This often brings these cats into conflict with humans. Today, there may be as few as 2,500 tigers left in the wild.

WHITE TIGER
This stunning color variety is a natural but rare occurrence in tigers from central India. Over 100 white tigers have been bred in zoos. One sighting of a tiger without stripes has also been recorded.

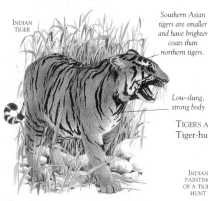

INDIAN TIGER

Southern Asian tigers are smaller and have brighter coats than northern tigers.

Low-slung, strong body

TIGERS AND PEOPLE
Tiger-hunting has a long history. Elephants were once used in these hunts because they gave a relatively safe vantage point for the hunter.

INDIAN PAINTING OF A TIGER HUNT

SOLITARY NIGHTTIME PROWLER
Tigers live alone in dense forests across Asia, where they normally stay hidden. Unlike most cats, tigers like water and spend a great deal of time swimming or just keeping cool.

GREAT CAT OF ASIA

There are about seven subspecies of tiger, all of which are endangered. These forms vary in size and color. The Siberian tiger is the largest and rarest, weighing up to 845 lb (384 kg). It can jump 40 ft (12 m) – over four times its body length.

Hair on cheeks is longer than rest of coat, particularly in older males.

White areas of fur on head

Razor-sharp canine teeth

SIBERIAN TIGER

REFERENCE
SECTION

CAT CLASSIFICATION

CLASSIFICATION IS a scientific system that arranges living things into groups according to features they share. The class of mammals encompasses more than 4,000 species of warm-blooded animals with hair. Within this class there are 20 different orders, one of which, the meat-eating carnivores, includes cats, dogs, and bears. The cat family, Felidae, is divided into three main genera, which include some 39 distinct cat species.

20 OTHER ORDERS, E.G., RODENTS, WHALES, HOOFED MAMMALS

PUMA

CHIMPANZEE

MAMMALIA
MAMMALS

FELIDAE
CATS

CARNIVORA
CARNIVORES

KEY:

☐ CLASS
☐ ORDER
☐ FAMILY
☐ GENERA
☐ SPECIES

THE ONZA: A NEW DISCOVERY?
In 1986, a new species of large, wild cat called the onza was thought to have been discovered in western Mexico. However, recent research has shown it to be a long-legged form of the puma. Nothing is known its numbers in the wild, or its precise distribution.

ONZA

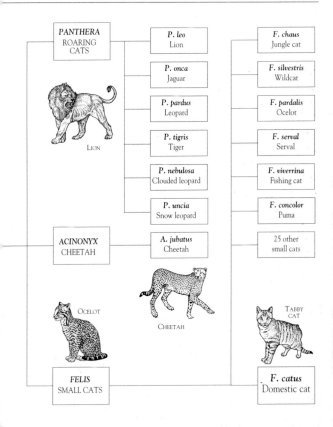

PANTHERA ROARING CATS	P. leo Lion	F. chaus Jungle cat
	P. onca Jaguar	F. silvestris Wildcat
	P. pardus Leopard	F. pardalis Ocelot
	P. tigris Tiger	F. serval Serval
	P. nebulosa Clouded leopard	F. viverrina Fishing cat
	P. uncia Snow leopard	F. concolor Puma
ACINONYX CHEETAH	A. jubatus Cheetah	25 other small cats
FELIS SMALL CATS		F. catus Domestic cat

LION

OCELOT

CHEETAH

TABBY CAT

ENDANGERED CATS

WILD CATS are under more threat today than ever before. Each year, many cats are killed for their fur. In some places, the big cats are killed because their bones, when ground up, are superstitiously believed to cure ill health. Those cats that survive face shrinking habitats as cities, farms, and roads encroach into wild areas. Development has become the biggest threat to the survival of many cats.

EXAMPLE	HABITAT	REASONS FOR DECLINE
TIGER	Scattered areas of forest reserves, mainly in India, Southeast Asia, China, and as far north as Siberia.	The tiger is heavily hunted for its bones, which are ground up to make medicines. It is also killed because of its threat to people and livestock. There may be as few as 2,500 in the wild.
MARGAY	Wooded forests of the Americas, from Mexico southward to Argentina, east of the Andes.	Until the 1980s, huge numbers of margays were hunted for their pelts. Their numbers have fallen dramatically in the southern part of their range. Forest clearance now poses another serious threat.
SNOW LEOPARD	Remote mountainous areas of central Asia and India, usually at very high altitude.	As tigers grow scarce, snow leopards are hunted to make remedies from their bones. They are also killed because they prey on livestock. There may be only 3,500 snow leopards left.

Example	Habitat	Reasons for decline
Iriomote cat	Ranges from the mountains down to the beaches of Iriomote Island, a Pacific island east of Taiwan.	Discovered in 1967, this cat lives only on the small Japanese island of Iriomote. Although it is now protected by law, hunting and habitat destruction have decreased its numbers to 80.
Asiatic lion	Confined to the scrub and thorn forests of the Gir Forest National Park in Gujarat, west-central India.	Once found all over Asia, the Asiatic lion was hunted almost to extinction in the early 1900s. Their numbers fell to 12, but have risen to 300 since their protection in the Gir reserve.
Scottish wildcat	Mountainous, forested Highlands area in the central and northern parts of Scotland.	Hunting began the Scottish wildcat's decline, but these cats are now protected. Today their greatest threat is interbreeding with domestic cats, which produces hybrid wildcats.
Clouded leopard	Densely forested areas of Southeast Asia, mainly in Java, Sumatra, Borneo, and Taiwan.	Destruction of their forest habitats is the major threat to these cats. They are also hunted for their striking, marbled fur. Pesticides, used in farming, may also be poisoning some cats.
Spanish lynx	Ranges from remote mountains to coastal areas in southwest Spain and neighboring parts of Portugal.	The decline of this species is mainly due to hunting, but also to its shrinking habitat. Lynxes are still trapped, and some are killed on roads. Their numbers are now fewer than 250.

CHOOSING A CAT

A CAT MAY LIVE for more than 15 years, and it needs a caring home for life. Once you have decided to make this commitment, you must choose the right companion. You may want to adopt an older cat, as kittens demand a lot of attention. However, kittens adapt easily to a new home.

Should show no evidence of pain when handled

THE HEALTHY KITTEN

A young kitten should not be taken from its mother before it is three months old. A healthy kitten is lively, playful, and alert, although it may sleep for long periods.

Body should be plump, but a potbelly may be a sign of roundworms.

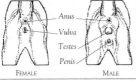

SEXING A KITTEN
The anus and penis in a male cat are farther apart than the anus and vulva in a female.

Anus

Vulva

Testes

Penis

FEMALE   MALE

You may want to have your kitten neutered when it reaches four to six months of age.

Legs should show no signs of lameness.

WHAT YOU SHOULD LOOK FOR

  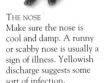

THE EARS
Check that the earflaps are not torn or bitten. Look inside the ears for excess wax or other discharge. A bad odor could indicate infection.

THE EYES
These should be clean, clear, and bright, with no signs of discharge. The inner eyelid (a white film) in the corner of the eye should not be visible.

THE NOSE
Make sure the nose is cool and damp. A runny or scabby nose is usually a sign of illness. Yellowish discharge suggests some sort of infection.

MOUTH AND GUMS
Carefully open the mouth to check that the teeth are not broken. The gums and tongue should be pink and healthy. The breath should be fresh.

THE COAT
Look for a clean, glossy coat. Dark specks are evidence of fleas. Any hair loss, particularly bald patches, could be an indication of ringworm.

THE REAR
Any stains on the rear are likely to mean the kitten has a digestive disorder. If you see what looks like small grains of rice, the kitten has tapeworms.

CARING FOR YOUR CAT

FOR THE MOST PART, cats can take care of themselves.
However, they have certain basic needs, as well as
individual demands, that you should be prepared for.
Even the most independent cats
sometimes need special care.

WHAT YOU MIGHT NEED

A basic range of equipment is
shown here. An indoor cat is
likely to require more equipment
than a cat that can go outside.

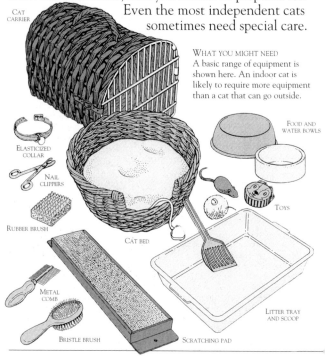

CAT
CARRIER

ELASTICIZED
COLLAR

NAIL
CLIPPERS

RUBBER BRUSH

CAT BED

FOOD &
WATER BOWLS

TOYS

METAL
COMB

BRISTLE BRUSH

SCRATCHING PAD

LITTER TRAY
AND SCOOP

FEEDING (FEED CAT AT THE SAME TIME AND PLACE AT LEAST TWICE A DAY)			
Type	Preparation	Value	Comments
Moist food (includes meat or fish, and cereal).	Serve straight from can into clean bowl.	Cats find this the tastiest type of prepared cat food.	Must be fresh; spoils quickly in hot weather.
Semimoist (includes soya, processed meat, and often sugar).	Open foil pack and serve into clean bowl.	Cats prefer softer texture to most dry cat foods.	The drier the food, the more water the cat needs to drink.
Dry food (includes dried, processed meat, and cereal).	Pour from box or packet into bowl.	Hard texture prevents tartar from forming on teeth and gums.	Lightest to carry and does not spoil easily.
Milk (either cow's milk or special milk for cats).	Pour from carton into clean bowl.	Valuable source of vitamins, calcium, and other minerals.	Cow's milk may cause diarrhea in some cats.
Fresh foods (egg, fish, meat, poultry, or cheese).	Should always be fresh. Cook before feeding to your cat.	Adds variety and interest to cat's diet. Good for convalescing cats.	These foods are not nutritionally balanced on their own.

GROOMING YOUR CAT

Grooming helps eliminate the problems of loose hairs around the home, hairballs, and fleas. As you are combing the fur you may see dark specks; these indicate that fleas are present. Groom your cat outdoors with a special fine-toothed comb to locate the fleas. Special flea sprays, powders, or collars can then be used to treat the cat.

Tangles can be removed with a metal comb.

COMMON HEALTH PROBLEMS

CATS ARE NORMALLY healthy, but they can be afflicted by various ailments. Most of a cat's illnesses can be prevented by vaccinations and check-ups at the vet. You can purchase veterinary insurance to cover your pet. In case of serious emergencies, contact a vet immediately.

INJURED CAT

ACCIDENTS ON THE ROAD

It is impossible to prevent a cat from crossing roads. Night is the most dangerous time, when a cat can be blinded by car headlights. If possible, keep your cat indoors after dark.

• If a cat has been hit by a car, carefully lift it out of danger. You must keep its body flat in case of internal injury. Place your hands under the cat's chest and pelvis, or use a sheet like a stretcher. Do not raise the cat's head.

• After an accident, a vet should always be called, since it is difficult to assess internal injuries. Make sure that the cat is kept warm and still.

DIGESTIVE PROBLEMS

There are many reasons for digestive upsets. Symptoms might include vomiting, loss of appetite or weight loss, diarrhea, or constipation.

• It is normal for cats to vomit occasionally, for example, if they have eaten grass. If vomiting occurs with diarrhea, or if any blood is present in the stools, contact a vet immediately.

• Watch out for the appearance of the third eyelid, or swelling or tenderness in the cat's abdomen. If any symptoms persist for more than 24 hours, a vet should be called.

• In cases of constipation, give your cat a teaspoonful of liquid paraffin in its food once a day for several days.

POISONING

Some medicines, such as aspirin, are fatal for cats. Household chemicals are also poisonous and should be stored safely away from your pets. Symptoms of poisoning include vomiting, convulsions, drooling, or collapse.

• Cats will drink car antifreeze even though it is highly toxic. In this case, rush the cat to the vet, who may be able to provide an antidote to block the effect of the poison.

• A cat's coat can become contaminated, and when it tries to clean itself the cat can be poisoned. If possible, wash the cat and wrap it in a towel so it cannot lick its fur. In severe cases, contact the vet.

WOUNDS AND BLEEDING

Cats may receive wounds in fights or be injured in other ways. If the cat is not in too much distress you should be able to attend to the wounds. Consult a vet if the injuries seem serious.

• In cases of severe bleeding, apply pressure on the wound with absorbent cotton gauze and wrap a bandage around it to keep it in place.

• Any bites or punctures should be carefully cleaned. Clip the fur around the wound and wash the area in warm salt water.

• An abscess may develop, which should burst after 24 hours if bathed frequently. Keep cleaning the wound. Antibiotics may be necessary.

PARASITES

A range of parasites, both internal and external, can infest cats. Fleas are the most common affliction. Kittens and cats that hunt a lot are most susceptible to internal parasites.

• Keep a close watch for fleas, ticks, and other pests in your cat's coat. You can treat your pet with sprays or powders. Clean the areas of your home, such as carpets and the cat's bedding, where fleas tend to breed.

• Typical symptoms of worms include weight loss, diarrhea, a potbellied appearance, or the cat excessively licking its behind. Your vet can prescribe tablets or deworming paste to treat the problem.

FIRST AID

SOME COMMON EMERGENCIES can be handled at home when your cat gets into trouble. However, if you suspect your cat needs further assistance, contact a vet without delay. It is useful to have a few first aid supplies at home for emergencies.

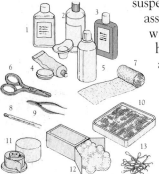

A BASIC FIRST AID KIT
1 Safe disinfectant. 2 Human eye wash.
3 Liquid paraffin (for cat constipation).
4 Antiseptic cream. 5 Antiseptic wash.
6 Round-ended scissors. 7 Bandages.
8 Rectal thermometer. 9 Tweezers.
10 Cotton gauze. 11 Adhesive dressing.
12 Cotton balls. 13 Cotton swabs.

TAKING A CAT'S TEMPERATURE
First, gently restrain the cat – otherwise it may bite and scratch. Lift the tail and insert a lubricated thermometer about 1 in (2.5 cm) into the anus. Hold it there for at least one minute. The temperature should be about 100°F (38.6°C).

Hold scruff of neck.

Try concealing the tablet in food.

GIVING PILLS
Open the cat's mouth, tip its head back, and place the pill as far back in the throat as possible. Then hold the mouth closed, stroking the throat until the cat swallows.

REMOVING FOREIGN BODIES
If splinters or other objects
become stuck between your
cat's toes you can remove
them using tweezers. Ask a
vet to remove anything
embedded in the pad since
this will be painful for the
cat and may cause bleeding.

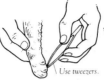

Use tweezers.

REMOVING FOREIGN BODY

Hold firmly.

DISINFECTING WOUND

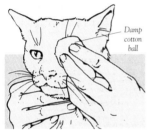

Damp cotton ball

TREATING THE EYES
If your cat has an eye infection, gently
wipe away discharge. Then carefully
apply eye drops or ointment and hold
the eyes closed for a few seconds.

BANDAGING MINOR WOUNDS
In case of a wound, first use pressure to
stop the bleeding. Then clean the area
and attach a gauze pad by wrapping a
bandage around it (not too tightly!).

CHECKING VITAL SIGNS
If a cat is unconscious, call
a vet immediately. Check
for breathing and pulse.
Feel for the heartbeat
below the cat's elbow on
the lower part of its chest.
If necessary, stimulate the
heart by pressing gently.

Watch for breathing.

CHECKING BREATHING

Heart rate should be 160–240 beats per minute.

Cat must be on right side.

CHECKING HEARTBEAT

UNDERSTANDING YOUR CAT

CATS COMMUNICATE vocally by purring, meowing, or hissing. They also express themselves with facial and body language. Domestic cats share much of their behavior with their wild cousins. Yet they have had to adapt to share their territories with other animals and people.

CLAIMING POSSESSION
When a cat rubs against objects it is marking its territory. Every cat has scent glands around its chin and near the rear of its body. Your cat may rub against your legs to claim you as its own.

PURRING IN CONTENTMENT
No one is certain how a cat makes its characteristic purring sound. It may be produced by vibrating membranes near the vocal cords in the throat. Purring normally indicates that a cat is relaxed and content; however, an ill or upset cat may also purr occasionally.

Ears perked up to collect information

Ears slightly forward but relaxed

Eyes half-closed in pleasure

ALERT
Something has caught this cat's attention. Its eyes are opened wide as it stares intently at a potential threat or prey. The cat pauses, assessing the intrusion, but remains vigilant.

CONTENT
Relaxed and trouble-free, this cat is settling down to sleep in comfortable surroundings. Its eyes are half-closed and not focusing specifically on anything. The cat may be purring.

Eyes watchful

Ears flattened

Pupils dilated in fear

Tongue arched in mouth

CURIOUS
The cat holds its ears forward to pick up sounds as it assesses the object of its curiosity. Its body language will show uncertainty (the tail may be flicking), which can easily switch to aggression.

AGGRESSIVE
To show extreme fear or anger, a cat flattens its ears and opens its mouth to bare its sharp teeth. The whiskers are held out, and the cat hisses fiercely to intimidate its enemy.

AMAZING CAT RECORDS

THERE IS NO SHORTAGE of remarkable facts about cats. Many of these arise from their long and colorful association with people. Cats also have many unique adaptations that have evolved over time.

SIZE

• Largest wild cat : Siberian tiger – up to 13 ft (4 m) from nose to tip of tail; can weigh up to 845 lb (384 kg).

• Smallest wild cat: Black-footed cat – 23 in (57.5 cm) from nose to tip of tail.

• Lightest wild cat: Rusty-spotted cat – weighs 3 lb (1.36 kg).

• Heaviest domestic cat: A male tabby from Australia weighed nearly 47 lb (21.3 kg) when he died in 1986.

• Lightest domestic cat: A Siamese cross weighed 1 lb 12 oz (0.79 kg) at two years old.

HISTORY

• Largest burial: 300,000 mummified cats were found in one ancient Egyptian tomb.

• Earliest cats in war: In 500 B.C., the Persians used cats as a shield against the Egyptians, who dared not kill their sacred animal.

• First cat liberation: In 1000 A.D., a Japanese decree freed all house cats to catch mice on farms.

• Most unusual use: In Britain, in the 14th–18th centuries, dead cats were built into the walls of houses to scare away mice.

UNUSUAL CATS

• Most unusual mutation: Domestic cats born with winglike flaps of skin on their backs. One Swedish cat had a "wingspan" of 23 in (59 cm).

• Most body parts: In 1975 in the US, a domestic cat was born with five legs, six paws, and 30 toes.

• Most unique: The one and only example of a "litigon" – the offspring of a lion and a tigon (itself a cross between a tiger and a lioness) – was born in a zoo in Calcutta, India.

HUNTING

• Best mouser: A tortoiseshell cat living in a whiskey distillery in Scotland. She killed 28,899 mice – three a day for 20 years.

• Most ferocious: The record number of people killed by a single cat is 84 by a lion, 400 by a leopard, and 436 by a tiger.

LIFESPAN

• Oldest domestic cat: A Sphynx called Granpa that lived to the age of 34 years and 2 months. He died in 1998.

• Oldest wild cat: A lion in Cologne Zoo in Germany that lived to be 29 years old. Lions in the wild generally live for only about 12 years.

FAME

• Most famous film star: Leo the MGM lion starred in many films and did stunts.

• Most famous fictional cats: The cat characters in T.S. Eliot's *Old Possum's Book of Practical Cats* (1939), on which the award-winning musical *Cats* is based.

FEATS

• Farthest traveler: A US Persian walked 1,500 miles (2,400 km) in 13 months to find her owner.

• Best climber: In 1950, a four-month-old kitten followed climbers to the top of the 14,691 ft (4,478 m) Matterhorn in the Alps.

FAMILY LIFE

• Best breeder: A tabby cat from Texas gave birth to 420 kittens in her life.

• Oldest mother: In 1987, a nonpedigree cat had two kittens at the age of 30 years.

• Most hazardous: The male lion of the pride may kill any lion cubs that are not his own.

MOST VALUABLE

• Most expensive meal: A Persian ate a diamond and ruby ring worth $4,800.

• Most valuable collection: A Texas farmer kept up to 1,400 cats on his farm.

• Most costly kittens: Savannah kittens may sell for $4,500 each.

Resources

When contacting any of these organizations for information, it may bring a quicker reply if you include a stamped, self-addressed envelope.

UNITED STATES

ORGANIZATIONS FOR CAT HEALTH

Alley Cat Allies
1801 Belmont Road NW
Washington, DC 20009

American Association of Feline Practitioners
200 4th Avenue North
Nashville, TN 37219

American Veterinary Medical Association
1931 North Meacham Rd.
Schaumburg, IL 60173

Animal Medical Center
510 East 62nd Street
New York, NY 10021

SHOW BODIES

These organizations can supply information on pedigree standards for cats, registration, and details about cat shows.

American Association of Cat Enthusiasts
P.O. Box 213
Pine Brook, NJ 07058

American Cat Association
8101 Katherine Avenue
Panorama City,
CA 91402

American Cat Fanciers' Association
P.O. Box 1949
Nixa, MO 65714

Cat Fanciers' Association, Inc.
P.O. Box 1005
Manasquan, NJ 08736

Cat Fanciers' Federation, Inc.
P.O. Box 661
Gratis, OH 45330

The International Cat Association
P.O. Box 2684
Harlingen, TX 78551

ORGANIZATIONS AGAINST ANIMAL CRUELTY

American Feline Society
204 W. 20th Street
New York, NY 10011

American Society for the Prevention of Cruelty to Animals (ASPCA)
424 East 92nd Street
New York, NY 10128

Cat Care Society
5786 West 6th Avenue
Lakewood, CO 80214

Humane Society of the United States
2100 L Street, NW
Washington, DC 20037

**National Cat
Protection Society**
6904 W. Coast Highway
Newport Beach,
CA 92663

Pet Pride
P.O. Box 1055
Pacific Palisades,
CA 90272

OTHER USEFUL ORGANIZATIONS

Cat Collectors
P.O. Box 150784
Nashville, TN 37215

**Cat Writers'
Association**
800 South 1417 #213
Sherman, TX 75090

Library Cat Society
P.O. Box 274
Moorhead, MN 56560

**People and
Cats Together**
P.O. Box 5477
Sherman Oaks,
CA 91413

ORGANIZATIONS FOR INFORMATION ON THE WORLD'S WILD CATS

**American Association
of Zoological Parks
and Aquariums**
The Conservation Center
7970-D Old Georgetown Rd.
Bethesda, MD 20814

**International Society
of Cryptozoology**
P.O. Box 43070
Tucson, AZ 85733
(For information on
unexplained cat sightings
worldwide)

**IUCN/SSC
Cat Specialist Group**
Thunstrasse 31, Muri b.
Bern 3074, Switzerland
(An international
organization specifically
formed to gather
information about cats)

**National Wildlife
Federation**
1400 16th Street NW
Washington, DC 20036

**World Wildlife Fund
(United States)**
1250 24th Street NW
Washington, DC 20037

CAT MAGAZINES

Cat Fancy
3 Burroughs
Irvine, CA 92618

Cats Magazine
P.O. Box 290037
Port Orange, FL 32129

Cat World International
P.O. Box 35635
Phoenix, AZ 85069

CANADA

**Canadian Cat
Association**
289 Rutherford Road S.,
#18
Brampton ON L6W 3R9

**World Wildlife Fund
(Canada)**
245 Eglinton Ave. East
Toronto ON M4P 3J1

Glossary

ADAPTATION
An evolutionary process by which living things adapt to their habitats.

AWN HAIR
Short, thick, bristly hair which lies underneath a cat's top coat.

BINOCULAR VISION
Using both eyes to focus on and judge the distance of an object.

BLOODLINE
The ancestors of a cat, stretching back over generations.

BREED
Cats that are similar to each other, based on a specific set of standards.

CAMOUFLAGE
Colors or markings that help animals blend into their surroundings.

CARNIVORE
An animal that eats the flesh of other animals.

CARPAL PADS
Antiskid pads found on the "wrists" of the cat's front legs.

CATTERY
A place where cats are bred or can board.

CLASSIFICATION
A system of organizing living things into groups according to features they have in common.

COBBY
A compact, rounded body shape in cats.

CROSS-BREEDING
Mating between two different breeds.

DOMINANT CHARACTERISTIC
A genetic characteristic that occurs in both parent and offspring.

DOUBLE COAT
Short, soft undercoat with a thick, resilient outer coat.

DOWN HAIR
Short, soft hair that grows in tufts and provides insulation.

EVOLUTION
A theory that explains how living things adapt and change over generations.

EXTINCTION
When a species ceases to exist, either naturally or through human interference.

FELINE
Member of the cat family, Felidae.

FERAL
A once-domestic cat that has reverted to living in the wild.

FLEHMENING
The grimace a cat makes when it draws air over the Jacobsen's organ in its mouth.

GROOMING
Licking and wiping of the fur to keep it clean and spread the cat's scent around its body.

GUARD HAIR
Long, coarse hairs that make up the cat's top coat. These carry the pattern of the fur.

HABITAT
The environment in which an animal lives.

HYBRID
Offspring that results from the breeding of different species.

INBREEDING
Breeding between relatives, which can cause genetic mutations in the offspring.

IN HEAT
The period in which a female cat looks for a partner to mate with.

JACOBSON'S ORGAN
An organ in the roof of a cat's mouth that is linked with the senses of smell and taste.

LITTER
All the kittens born to a mother in a single birth.

MOLTING
The (usually) seasonal shedding of the coat.

MUTATION
A genetic change that can be either harmless or unhealthy.

NEUTERING
Surgically removing the means of reproduction.

NOCTURNAL
Active at night.

NONPEDIGREE
A cat that has not been specially bred to achieve certain standards.

PADS
Tough, leathery, furless cushions on the underside of a cat's feet.

PAPILLAE
The tiny, pointed hooks on a cat's tongue that give the tongue its rough surface.

PARASITES
Animals, like fleas, that live off other creatures.

PEDIGREE
The written record of the line of descent of a purebred cat.

POINTED
Fur pattern with darker areas on the head, ears, legs, paws, and tail.

POLYDACTYL
A cat born with more toes than is normal.

PREDATOR
An animal that hunts to catch the food it needs to survive.

PRIDE
A group of lions, usually closely related, that live and hunt together.

QUEEN
Unneutered female cat.

RANGE
The area in which an individual animal or a species lives.

RETRACTABLE CLAWS
Claws that are sheathed when a cat is relaxed, and extended only when necessary.

SELECTIVE BREEDING
Breeding of animals by humans in order to achieve desired features.

SPECIES
A group of similar animals that can breed together to produce fertile young.

SPRAYING
When a cat (usually male) sprays urine to mark its territory.

TABBY
Dark coat markings that can be stripes, blotches, or spots.

TAPETUM LUCIDUM
Mirrorlike layer of cells behind the cat's retina. These cells reflect light for good night vision.

TERRITORY
Area that a particular cat occupies and defends against other cats.

THIRD EYELID
Membrane underneath the outer eyelid that only appears when the cat is injured or ill.

TICKING
A fur color distinguished by bands of color on each hair.

TOM
Unneutered male cat.

WHISKERS
Specialized, stiff hairs with highly sensitive nerves at their roots.

Index

159

Acknowledgments

Dorling Kindersley would like to thank:
Hilary Bird for the index; Carlton Hibbert, Myfanwy Hancock, and Kate Eagar for design assistance; Caroline Potts and Robert Graham for picture research assistance; Ray Rogers, Kristin Ward, and Connie Mersel for editorial assistance.

Photographs by:
Jane Burton, Steve Gorton, Marc Henrie, Colin Keates, Dave King, Tracy Morgan, Tim Ridley, Jerry Young

Illustrations by:
Gill Ellsbury, Angelica Elsebach, Chris Forsey, Craig Gosling (Indiana University Medical Illustration Department), Kenneth Lilly, Stanley Cephas Johnson, Janos Marffy, Malcolm McGregor, John Temperton, Ann Winterbotham, John Woodcock, Dan Wright

Picture credits: t = top b = bottom
c = center l = left r = right
The publisher would like to thank the following for their kind permission to reproduce the photographs:

Adams Picture Library 109tr; Alaska State Library/Early Prints, 01-2034 129tr; Alison Ashford 92tr; Aquila/ M.W. Fowles 17tl, M.C. Wilfes 81tl; Bridgeman Art Library/British Museum 2cl, 130tl, 132br; The British Library, Oriental and India Office Collections 123 bl; Hilda Blackmore 107bl; Chanan 88/89, 89tr, 100l; Paul Casey/CSCA 97tl; Bruce

Coleman 120l, 120cr, 123tl, 126bl, 131cr; Mary Evans 56tl, 64tr, 73tl, 77cr, 106tl, 114cl; ET Archive 87tl; Robert Harding Picture Library 58tr, 66tl, 94bl, 104tr, Rainbird/Derrick Nitty 12l; Martin Harvey/Gallo Images 112cl; Marc Henrie 63tl, 70tr, 75br, 103tl; Michael Holford 98l; Hulton Deutsch Collection 88tl; Image Bank/Joseph Van Os 97tr, 110tl, 119c, Guido Alberto Rossi 125tl; Larry Johnson 48; JumanjiBengals.com 112bl; John Massey-Stewart 107tr, Natural History Museum 3cl, 14, 15tl, 15b; Nature Photographers/Michael Gore 42r, 43tl, 131tl; NHPA 125tr, Planet Earth/Carol Farneti 27tr, 31tr, 127tl, Jonathan Scott 35tr, 36tl, Anup and Manoj Shah 33tr, 127cr; Pobjoy Mint Ltd 54tl; Tony Stone Images/Paul Chesley 69tr, Jeanne Drake 16tl, 118b, 119c, Ian Murphy 124/125, Mark Peterson 39b, Manoj Shah 125br, 128bl, 133; Tonda M. Straede 80l; World Pictures 105tr; Tetsu Yamazaki 49, 51b, 55tr, 89tr, 94cr, 98br, 99r, 113tr; Jerry Young front cover br, 10/11, 40/41b, 67tl; Zefa 25tr, 41t, 90tr, 121tr.

Every effort has been made to trace the copyright holders and we apologize in advance for any unintentional omissions. We would be pleased to insert the appropriate acknowledgment in any subsequent edition of this publication.

All other images © Dorling Kindersley
For further information see:
www.dkimages.com